Schools and disruptive pupils

Schools and disruptive pupils

David Galloway
Tina Ball
Diana Blomfield
Rosalind Seyd

Longman
London and New York

Longman Group Limited
Longman House, Burnt Mill, Harlow
Essex CM20 2JE, England
Associated companies throughout the world

*Published in the United States of America
by Longman Inc., New York*

© Longman Group Limited 1982

First published 1982
Second impression 1983

British Library Cataloguing in Publication Data

Schools and disruptive pupils.
   1. Problem children – England
   I. Galloway, David
   371.94′0942   LC4801
   ISBN 0–582–49707–8

Library of Congress Cataloging in Publication Data

Main entry under title:

Schools and disruptive pupils.

   Bibliography: p.
   Includes index.
   I. Problem children – Education.   I. Galloway,
David.
LC4801.S34   1982   371.93   81–15601
ISBN 0–582–49707–8   AACR2

Printed in Great Britain by
Butler & Tanner Ltd, Frome and London

Contents

Acknowledgements

The research in Sheffield LEA described in this book was funded by the Department of Education and Science. We gratefully acknowledge the Department's support, and the constructively critical advice of the Department's officers. Our work could not have taken place without the encouragement and support of Mr G. M. A. Harrison, Chief Education Officer, and his colleagues in Sheffield Education Department. In particular, we gratefully acknowledge the help of Mr John Mann, former Deputy Education Officer, and Dr W. R. Kneen, Second Deputy (Schools). Our inquiries had their origin in work carried out by Sheffield Education Department's Psychological Service, under the guidance of Mr David Loxley. The critical support of Mr Loxley and his colleagues was extremely helpful. Mr Brian Wilcox, Senior Adviser in Sheffield Education Department, gave invaluable assistance throughout the research programme. Helpful advice was also received from Professor John Roach, Chairman of Sheffield School and Home Project Advisory Committee, and from his colleagues in the University of Sheffield, Dr P. Poppleton, Sir Edward Britton and Professor R. Loynes. Finally, but by no means least, we are grateful to the necessarily anonymous schools, teachers and pupils whose cooperation made this book possible. The willingness of schools to cooperate with an investigation into such sensitive educational issues speaks for itself.

We are indebted to the following for permission to reproduce copyright material:

The Journal, Trends in Education, for a table from the article 'Exclusion and Suspension from School' by David Galloway: SET Research Information for Teachers for extracts from the article 'Disruptive Pupils' by David Galloway.

For deciphering and typing the manuscript we thank Miss Margot Johnstone, Mrs Gwen Wright, Mrs Jean Pope and Miss Jane Van der Beck.

Disclaimers

The views expressed in this book are the authors' own. They should not be taken to reflect those of any individuals or institutions who cooperated with the inquiries described in the book, nor of Sheffield LEA.

In describing our results, we have been conscious of the need for accuracy, while preserving the anonymity of the schools, teachers and pupils involved. When presenting case histories, both of schools and pupils, and when quoting teachers or pupils verbatim, we have changed names, abbreviation of names, nicknames and other identifying characteristics.

We have used the male gender when writing in general terms about head-teachers, pupils and teachers responsible for special groups. We have used the female gender when writing in general terms about other teachers, parents and other professionals.

Introduction: who are the disruptive pupils?

Background

The changing climate in society and in schools
For twenty-five years from the end of the Second World War, education was in a state of more or less continual expansion throughout the English-speaking world. Important developments took place in virtually every area of education. The climate was one of optimistic confidence in the value, and the necessity, of education in promoting economic growth and equality of opportunity.

The first half of the 1970s saw this expansion falter. In the second half, economic recession, political uncertainty and, at least in the UK, declining birth-rates saw the expansion grind towards a halt. There are depressingly clear signs that the 1980s may see it reversed. It is a sad paradox that in this climate of uncertainty, suspicion and retrenchment, almost the only undisputed growth area in education should be provision for problem pupils.

At least in England and North America, a glance at the agenda for the AGM of any major teaching union reveals alarm at the supposedly growing tide of violence in schools. That disruptive behaviour has increased, is increasing, and will continue to increase, has passed into educational folklore. But has this belief any basis in fact? We have no reliable way of comparing the prevalence of disruptive behaviour over prolonged periods of time. We shall see in Chapter 1, however, that the limited available evidence lends no support to the notion of a large increase in the number of pupils presenting problems, or in the severity of the problems they present. What is less controversial is that anxiety about problem behaviour has increased dramatically in the last decade. Three reasons are often put forward for this.

1. Disruptive behaviour in schools is the inevitable manifestation of increased violence, or at least of increased reporting of violence, in the world as a whole. This is reflected, for example, in television coverage of Northern Ireland, of aeroplane hijackings and of the

armed occupation of embassies. Never before has violence been so visible.

2. Rightly or wrongly, teachers feel that their achievements are being questioned and their autonomy threatened. The 'Great Debate' on education initiated by James Callaghan as Prime Minister (1976) not only reflected the developing climate of scepticism about the aims and achievements of schools but also contributed to it. The establishment of the Assessment of Performance Unit by the Department of Education and Science reflected the same climate. Feeling themselves under attack by politicians and the media, it is not surprising that teachers in turn should publicise the problems which prevent them attaining the high standards to which they, and society, aspire. Disruptive behaviour in the classroom is only one of these, yet is almost guaranteed to arouse public sympathy for teachers and indignation against the offenders.

3. Existing services appear to have failed to solve the problem, even though expansion in these services has been as great as in any area of education. As we see in Chapter 1, the period since the last war has seen a huge increase in the number of special school places. The same period has seen a similar increase in the ranks of child psychiatrists, social workers responsible for children, educational psychologists and educational welfare officers – a 'veritable army' of helping professionals (Reynolds and Murgatroyd 1977). Yet in spite of these developments, demand for special school places for disruptive pupils continues to exceed supply. Moreover, teachers in many areas continue to complain of extensive delays when they seek advice about disruptive pupils or 'treatment' for them.

There may be some truth in each of these three reasons for the increase in anxiety, or anger, about disruptive pupils. However, we shall see later that at least one of them is based on a fundamental misunderstanding of the nature of the problem. The climate of opinion in society which has witnessed, if not caused, the phenomenon is nevertheless important not only for understanding current approaches to the problem, but also for recognising why so many of them have proved unsuccessful.

Different approaches

One rather obvious approach to the problem of disruptive behaviour is to create a climate inimical to its development in the first place. This approach focuses on the school as a social and educational institution which can create its own ethos of stability. The difficulty is that all teachers would cheerfully agree with this as an ideal. The questions are: how, and at what price? Many teachers feel that the real problem, in practice, is to find an appropriate reaction to disruptive behaviour when it *has* occurred.

Treatment and containment

With few exceptions, existing work with disruptive pupils falls into two groups, separated as much by their ideology as by their methods. A 'liberal' philosophy emphasises the importance of a caring pastoral care system in the school, which recognises the stresses to which disruptive pupils are exposed both at school and at home. 'Liberal' approaches are also optimistic about the value of treatment and support services such as educational psychology or social work. In contrast, a more 'traditional' philosophy advocates a more direct policy towards disruptive pupils, emphasising the need to control their activities so that the cooperative majority may benefit from what the school has to offer. We should, however, note that both approaches are essentially pupil-orientated. In other words, the individual is the focus for attention, rather than the school or classroom in which the disruption occurs.

Prevention

Neither of the two philosophies summarised above is inconsistent with the notion of prevention. Indeed, an essential element in the pastoral care and discipline systems of most secondary schools is their emphasis on tackling problems at an early stage, if not preventing them in the first place. Unfortunately, the way in which pastoral care and discipline systems are organised often reduces their effectiveness in preventing disruptive behaviour. A more immediate point, is that here too the emphasis is primarily on the individual pupil, or group of pupils.

An alternative is to concentrate attention on the social and learning environment. The aim is to give pupils greater opportunity for achievement and success, with a corresponding reduction in opportunity for the boredom and alienation which are so often associated with disruptive behaviour. The rationale here is that aspects of a school's curriculum and social organisation can create, or at least contribute to, the very problems which teachers and members of the support services subsequently spend a great deal of time and energy trying – often unsuccessfully – to solve. In Chapter 4 we review the evidence that schools do in fact influence the amount of disruptive behaviour in their pupils. Later, in Chapters 6 and 7, we examine in more detail some of the processes which may mediate this influence.

The need for an integrated approach
It appears, then, that existing approaches to disruptive behaviour differ sharply in two respects: (a) the emphasis they place on treatment as opposed to containment; (b) the emphasis they place on the individual as opposed to the school. Another way of expressing these distinctions is in terms of psychological and sociological influences.

Attempts to help the individual imply belief in a psychological model, based on the view that the individual's disruptive behaviour results from problems which can be treated. These problems may lie in the pupil, in his family, in his school or more commonly in an interaction between all three. Less 'child-centred' approaches based on the principles of punishment or containment are also based on a psychological model. Implicit in these approaches is the belief that the recalcitrant individual will respond to punishment, or that he is so hardened in his attitudes that containment offers the only solution, when treatment and punishment have both failed.

In contrast, attempts to modify the school environment so that it caters more satisfactorily for potentially disruptive pupils emphasise sociological processes within the school. Much recent work on the influence of school climate, or the 'hidden curriculum', may be seen as an attempt to identify the extent to which a school's rules and organisation are compatible with its stated goals. Thus, the emphasis is placed on the educational and social context in which the pupil must work and play, not on the individual himself.

Unfortunately there have so far been few serious attempts to integrate sociological and psychological approaches. As we argue, throughout the book, many disruptive pupils do have exceptional personal needs which cannot be ignored in any comprehensive treatment plan. Equally important though, is the fact that disruptive behaviour is a chronically stressful and time-consuming problem in some schools, while at others with similar pupils, this is not the case. Responses to disruptive behaviour must not only recognise the importance of factors in the pupil and his background, but also the relevance of factors in the school itself.

Problems of definition

Differing perceptions
Most teachers have a fairly well-defined idea of what constitutes disruptive behaviour. Similarly, they can identify the disruptive pupils in their classes without much difficulty. The trouble is that they have

different ideas about what constitutes disruptive behaviour, and identify different pupils.

There are two issues. One is that many pupils behave in different
ways, depending on their teacher and the school they are attending.
Experienced teachers can generally think of pupils with a hair-raising
record of misbehaviour who presented no further problems following
a change of school. Similarly, many pupils are disruptive only with
certain teachers. The second issue is related to this, and concerns the
teacher's tolerance level for different forms of behaviour. The point is
not simply that teachers vary in what they find irritating, so that a
'healthy extrovert' to one teacher is a 'noisy disrupter' to another. Just
as important, each individual varies in what she finds irritating. Behaviour that is mildly annoying on Tuesday morning may be the last
straw on Friday afternoon. Deviance, like beauty, lies in the eye of
the beholder.

Subjective reality

From the harassed teacher's point of view, disruptive behaviour can
appear irrational, unpredictable, abnormal. Yet when the incident is
analysed from a different point of view – that of the pupil – it frequently seems rational, predictable, normal.

The point is not that the teacher's reaction is unreasonable – from
her point of view it is eminently reasonable. The point is simply that
calling behaviour disruptive makes a value judgement, but does not
describe it. Supposedly objective statements cannot satisfactorily overcome this problem. 'Peter deliberately bumped into the pupil next to
him, knocking his books on the floor', for example, describes an event
observed by the teacher. The event was undoubtedly disruptive, yet
Peter's action has to be seen in the light of previous events between
him and his neighbour. The teacher's reaction is equally important,
since this may, in some circumstances, be as disruptive to the class as
the incident itself. A satisfactory definition of disruptive behaviour
must not only acknowledge the subjective nature of the concept, but
also recognise the teacher's importance. Behaviour which one teacher
is able to ignore without interrupting the lesson can escalate into a major confrontation with another teacher. We shall see that this has important implications for support networks within a school.

Are disruptive pupils maladjusted?

The concept of maladjustment is frequently invoked to justify removing disruptive pupils from ordinary lessons, whether for treatment or
for other reasons, but does little to clarify what is meant by disruptive

behaviour. Following the 1944 Education Act, the Handicapped Pupils and School Health Service Regulations (Ministry of Education 1945) described maladjusted pupils as those 'who show evidence of emotional instability or psychological disturbance, and who require special educational treatment in order to effect their personal, social and educational readjustment'.

Unfortunately this definition is vague to the point of being meaningless. Apart from the obvious difficulty that the terms 'emotional instability' and 'psychological disturbance' require as much clarification as maladjustment itself, it is hard to see what sort of special *educational* treatment is appropriate for children with personal and/or social problems.

Maladjustment is not a category in the most widely used classification systems in child psychiatry (Rutter 1965; Rutter et al. 1969). The chief function of the term, in fact, is to provide a label under which special education may be provided under the 1944 Education Act (Graham and Rutter 1970). Galloway and Goodwin (1979) accept this point of view, but go further, arguing that maladjustment is a hotchpotch term for describing *any* child whose teachers demand his removal from school following behaviour which they feel unable or unwilling to tolerate. This assessment is not invalidated by the fact that many children labelled maladjusted are emotionally withdrawn and show a wide range of 'neurotic' behaviour without being overtly disruptive. These children still have a disturbing effect on their teachers. They are regarded as maladjusted either if it is felt that their presence is too unsettling to the rest of the class or to their teacher, or if it is felt that they themselves could be helped by a special school.

It is clear from this discussion of maladjustment that *all* severely disruptive pupils *could* be called maladjusted, if any useful purpose would be served by doing so. In practice, of course, they only receive this label when special schooling is being seriously considered. Very few pupils are ever suspended from primary schools following disruptive behaviour. One obvious reason for this is that they can be transferred to a special school for maladjusted pupils before suspension becomes necessary. The only age-group of pupils in ordinary schools for whom few, if any, special school places are available is fourteen- to sixteen-year-olds. It is no coincidence that the majority of disruptive pupils suspended from school are in this age-group. Difficult pupils at primary schools are called maladjusted and referred to special schools. In Chapters 2 and 3 we report evidence from a survey in Sheffield that difficult pupils in their fourth and fifth years at secondary schools are liable to be called disruptive and suspended.

Similar difficulties arise when asking whether disruptive pupils should be regarded as psychiatrically disturbed. The answer depends almost entirely on how psychiatric disorder is defined. In an important series of studies described in Chapter 1, Rutter and Graham (1968) define psychiatric disorder as: 'abnormalities of emotions, behaviour or relationships which are developmentally inappropriate, and of sufficient duration and severity to cause persistent suffering or handicap to the child and/or distress or disturbance to the family or community'. They add, however, that: 'our use of the term does not involve any concept of disease, nor does it necessarily assume that psychiatrists are the right people to treat such disorders'. There is little doubt that this definition encompasses the majority of severely disruptive pupils, yet it is doubtful whether any useful practical purpose would be served by regarding disruptive pupils as just one group of psychiatrically disordered children. More important, we would still be no closer to agreement on a definition of disruptive behaviour as such.

Use of the term 'disruptive behaviour' in this book
Although the tiny minority whose behaviour results in their suspension from school have attracted most publicity, there is little doubt that these pupils represent the tip of the iceberg. Children's behaviour at school does not fall into two neat groups of normal or disruptive. It consists of a continuum, from extremely cooperative to totally unacceptable. Few children consistently occupy the same point on the continuum; their behaviour changes as their teachers, their age and their family circumstances change.

Thus, a wide range of behaviour may be regarded as disruptive. For present purposes, disruptive behaviour is defined as any behaviour which appears problematic, inappropriate and disturbing to teachers. This is broadly consistent with Rutter and Graham's concept of psychiatric disorder, but emphasises the subjective nature of the term. One teacher may be unaffected by behaviour which another finds inappropriate and disturbing.

Scope of the book

The root causes of disruptive behaviour may or may not lie in the structure of society, but that is a controversy with which this book is not concerned. The reason is simple. Teachers cannot change the society in which their pupils live (though their pupils will be changing society, for better or worse, in twenty or thirty years' time). In contrast, teachers *can* change their schools and there is now ample evidence that schools have a much greater influence on children's lives than was once supposed.

The aim of this book is to describe the nature and prevalence of disruptive behaviour in schools, and to discuss possible solutions to the problems it presents. The book draws on previously published research, supplemented by results of a two-year study of severely disruptive pupils in Sheffield. This study was carried out with financial assistance from the Department of Education and Science. It included a detailed survey of pupils who had been suspended from school, and a descriptive study of schools which had established a special group to cater for their problem pupils and schools which had quite consciously decided not to establish any such group.

The book is therefore concerned with a range of disruptive behaviour, but discusses this in a wider educational context. Attention is paid to the most severely disruptive minority, but emphasis on the school's potential influence over its pupils' behaviour makes clear that disruptive behaviour cannot be considered in isolation from the organisation and work of the school as a whole. The first three chapters define the extent and nature of the problem. The fourth takes a critical look at existing assessment and treatment facilities. This is followed by a detailed examination of some school-based procedures for reducing disruptive behaviour. Finally, we review the implications of existing information about this problem for schools and for LEA support services.

Chapter 1

An increasing problem – or just increasing provision?

Historical background

There is nothing new about violent and disruptive behaviour in schools. In the last century Charles Dickens publicised the educational standards at some independent schools in *Nicholas Nickleby*. At other, more well-known schools, riots by pupils led to intervention by the army (Gathorne-Hardy 1977). It helps to remember this background of instability in an age when a request by the head-teacher of a comprehensive school for assistance from the local police in dealing with a disturbance is likely to be accepted gratefully, even gleefully, by the press and by some politicians as evidence of deteriorating standards and impending chaos.

No one is quite sure exactly when the golden age of high educational standards and cooperative pupil behaviour existed. It was obviously not in the last century, when school attendance was, at best, erratic (Pallister 1969), and the available evidence on violence between pupils, and between teachers and pupils, makes the most hair-raising accounts of misbehaviour at today's secondary schools seem like Sunday school in suburbia. Nor, apparently, did the golden age exist between the two world wars. In a study of elementary schools in London, McFie (1934) reported a remarkable 46 per cent of pupils as showing one or more of four 'behaviour deviations'. These were timidity or lack of sociability, behaviour disorders such as truancy or stealing, habit disorders such as nail-biting or incontinence, and scholastic difficulties which were not attributable to mental deficiency. Four years later, Milner (1938) surveyed five schools run by the Girls Public Day School Trust, and found that teachers put forward 17 per cent of the girls for interview on account of their difficult behaviour.

In case it is thought that English children were uniquely deviant, or their teachers uniquely critical, similar findings were reported from North America. Haggerty (1925) reported that teachers in one school district reported undesirable behaviour in over 50 per cent of their

1

pupils. The most frequently reported problems were 'disinterest in school work, cheating, lying and tardiness'. Subsequent studies reviewed by Uger (1938) confirmed Haggerty's results. These studies also demonstrated that teachers tended to identify as problems the pupils who defied their authority or consistently refused to work. Conversely, they tended to overlook the shy, unsociable or timid child who did not threaten classroom order and stability. In this respect, these early studies anticipate the results of more recent work which distinguishes between 'conduct disorders', or overt, acting-out forms of behaviour, and 'neurotic disorders', or emotional problems which cause the child a great deal of distress but do not impinge in any overtly challenging way on others.

Recent surveys

Surveys of violent and disruptive behaviour
Teachers are often reluctant to admit that they have disciplinary problems, for fear of appearing incompetent in their colleagues' eyes. Similarly, head-teachers may also be reluctant to admit to outsiders that their school has problems. One effect of this understandable caution is that many surveys on the prevalence of disruptive behaviour achieve poor response rates, thus reducing their potential usefulness. A good example is Lowenstein's (1975) survey on behalf of the National Association of Schoolmasters. He sent all members a questionnaire on the prevalence of violent and disruptive behaviour, but obtained adequately completed returns from only 18 per cent of secondary school teachers and 5 per cent of primary teachers.

The low response rate unfortunately meant that Lowenstein's results could be regarded as of little more than anecdotal interest. Bearing this crucial limitation in mind, his completed questionnaires indicated an average of 0.53 violent incidents per 100 primary school pupils, and 0.64 incidents per 100 secondary school pupils. Lowenstein defined violence as: 'fairly vicious attacks on other pupils or members of the school staff'. He defined disruptive behaviour as: 'any behaviour short of physical violence which interferes with the teaching process, and/or upsets the normal running of the school'. Here, too, he found higher rates in secondary schools, an average of 4.45 incidents per 100 pupils, compared with 1.62 reported by primary teachers. Lowenstein's survey confirmed other evidence noted in this chapter, that violent and disruptive behaviour is more common among boys than girls. Within secondary schools, pupils aged fifteen or over presented most problems. He noted that size of school did not appear important, confirming Galloway's (1976a, b) evidence on persistent unauthorised absence from school.

Similar objections apply to a survey of violence in primary and secondary schools by the Association of Education Committees (Hansard 1975) as applied to Lowenstein's survey. Evidence in this survey was obtained from chief education officers rather than from individual schools. The difficulty here is that policy on reporting violence to the chief education officer varies from area to area and from school to school (Grunsell 1979). It is therefore difficult to know how much confidence to place in evidence reported in Parliament from 60 per cent of the completed questionnaires. The results indicated a lower rate of violent behaviour than reported by Lowenstein, but confirmed his impression that the problem was more common in secondary schools. Just over 13 per cent of secondary schools, for example, reported at least one incident of violence between pupils, compared with 2 per cent of primary schools. Violence towards teachers was much less common.

The best that can be said of these surveys is that they illustrate certain aspects of the problem. They do not provide an acceptable picture of the prevalence of violent or disruptive behaviour nor do they adequately place such behaviour within a broader educational or social context. In the absence of more systematic studies we must turn for evidence to the major epidemiological and longitudinal studies, which sought evidence on a wider range of behavioural problems than disruptive behaviour.

Other evidence

The Warnock Report on special education (DES 1978) concluded that up to 25 per cent of pupils would need some form of special educational help at some stage in their school career. Unfortunately the report did not indicate how many of these pupils would present substantial behavioural problems, but it is possible to form some idea from other research on which Warnock based her conclusions.

The National Child Development Study investigated the health, educational attainments and behaviour of all children born in one week of March 1958. At the age of seven each child's teacher was asked to complete an early version of the Bristol Social Adjustment Guide (Stott 1963). In this the teacher reads a large number of statements about the child's behaviour, and underlines the ones which describe him most accurately. From the results, Davie et al. (1972) concluded that teachers regarded 64 per cent of the children as stable, 22 per cent as unsettled and 14 per cent as maladjusted. The extent to which maladjusted children are also disruptive, or vice versa, was discussed in the Introduction. It is worth adding, however, that all pupils regarded as maladjusted on the Bristol Guides would also have a disruptive effect on their teachers, though not always because of overt, outwardly directed behaviour.

In the final school-age follow-up to the National Child Development Study, when the pupils were sixteen, Rutter's (1967) behaviour questionnaire was preferred to the Bristol Social Adjustment Guide. In the behaviour questionnaire, the teacher is given twenty-six statements about a pupil, such as 'is often disobedient', or 'often tells lies', and states whether each statement certainly applies to the child, applies somewhat, or does not apply. Fogelman (1976) did not report the number of pupils with high scores that indicated possible psychiatric disorder as defined by Michael Rutter's team (see below). He did, however, report that the statement: 'is often disobedient' applied at least to some extent to 18 per cent of the pupils. Similarly, the statement: 'irritable, quick to "fly off the handle" ' applied at least to some extent to 20 per cent of the pupils. As might be expected from other work, he noted that nailbiting, solitary and 'fussy' behaviour were more often reported by parents than by teachers.

The strength of the National Child Development Study lay in its size and its national coverage. The weakness inherent in this approach was that it had to rely heavily on screening techniques completed by professional personnel on the spot. A more detailed, and in some ways scientifically more rigorous picture of the prevalence of disruptive behaviour in schools emerges from local studies confined to one geographical area.

Shepherd et al. (1971) studied over 6,000 children attending Buckinghamshire schools in 1961. Among other things, teachers were given twenty-one statements, for example: 'often tells lies', or 'not interested in school work' and asked to underline the ones which applied to the survey children. Teachers noted no behaviour problems for just over half of the children, but boys were more likely to have at least one item marked than girls. As in other surveys, girls were more often rated as quiet or withdrawn, while boys were more often reported as aggressive, lacking interest, uncooperative, lying and stealing. Across the whole age-range, only 4 per cent of boys and nearly 2 per cent of girls were said to be uncooperative in class, but there was a marked increase in prevalence among fourteen- and fifteen-year-olds. The survey provided strong evidence that behaviour problems in school are associated with poor attainments.

The most detailed epidemiological and longitudinal studies of behaviour problems in English children were carried out in the Isle of Wight (Rutter et al. 1970) and in an inner London borough (Rutter et al. 1975a, 1975b). These studies investigated aspects of the pupils' health, educational attainments and family backgrounds in addition to their behaviour. The inner London borough contained a substantial number of immigrant children, (mainly West Indian). In order to draw valid comparisons between indigenous children in London and the Isle of Wight, evidence about the immigrant children was reported separately (Rutter et al. 1974, 1975c).

As a screening procedure, teachers were asked to complete Rutter's behaviour questionnaire mentioned above. Subsequently children were selected for intensive study on the basis of high questionnaire scores, and compared with a randomly selected control group. Their mothers were also interviewed for two to three hours by a social scientist or psychiatrist, using an interview schedule of known reliability (Graham and Rutter 1968a).

As might perhaps be expected, far more children were regarded as deviant in London than the Isle of Wight, on the basis of high scores on the teachers' behaviour questionnaire (19% and 11% respectively). An important incidental finding was that parents expressed concern about roughly the same number of children as teachers, but there was surprisingly little overlap between the groups. Children who were disruptive at school were *not* always regarded as problems at home, nor vice versa. To some extent the relatively small overlap between the two groups resulted from teachers identifying more overtly disturbing pupils, while parents identified a larger number of withdrawn children. This, of course, was consistent with Uger's (1938) earlier suggestion in North America and with results of the National Child Development Study. It did, however, raise the possibility that difficult behaviour at school might result from tensions at school, rather than from difficulties outside the school or constitutional problems within the child. It also suggested that teachers might not recognise signs of disturbance that did not involve overtly disruptive behaviour.

The number of children identified as deviant from the teachers' questionnaire is probably more important for present purposes than the number subsequently diagnosed as showing 'clinically significant' signs of psychiatric disorder, as defined in the Introduction. The number of children showing signs of psychiatric disorder in each area was calculated from the numbers identified from the control group and from the group selected by screening. Here too, roughly twice as many London children were identified as on the Isle of Wight (25%, compared with 12%). The higher London rate applied to both boys and girls, but was more noticeable in girls, mainly because of the high number of London girls whose problems were confined to the home, and were therefore not selected by the teachers' questionnaire.

Two points should be made about the results of these surveys. First, the fact that a pupil was regarded in the surveys as showing clinically significant signs of psychiatric disorder did not necessarily imply any concept of disease or illness, nor did it imply the necessity for psychiatric treatment. The second point is that the higher rate of behaviour problems reported by London teachers does not *per se* tell us anything about the cause or nature of these problems.

Information from the schools and from the pupils' families, however, showed conclusively that the greater prevalence of deviant behaviour in London was associated with higher rates of disadvantage both in the children's schools and in their families. Rutter and Quinton (1977) concluded that the difference between the two areas in child psychiatric disorder was entirely attributable to differences in family and school conditions. The school's influence was subsequently investigated in greater detail. The results of this study are described in Chapter 4.

Developmental aspects, or: the myth of early intervention

We shall see in Chapter 4 that many behaviour problems in children appear to improve spontaneously without formal treatment. Two more immediate points are whether disruptive behaviour becomes more prevalent in any particular age-group, and whether it is possible to prevent serious problems from arising by providing more efficient treatment or support services when the pupils are younger.

At least one problem does undoubtedly become a great deal more common in adolescence. This is unauthorised absence from school, the prevalence of which remains stable throughout the primary school years, but rises steadily in secondary schools, with a sharp peak in the final year of compulsory education (Galloway 1976a). These pupils are certainly disruptive in terms of the time spent investigating the reasons for their absence, and there is further evidence that teachers find their behaviour unacceptable when they do attend (Berg et al. 1978).

Such conclusions as can be drawn from the low response rate in Lowenstein's survey suggest that violent and severely disruptive incidents are indeed more prevalent in the final two years of compulsory education. It is not, however, clear whether the incidents themselves become more common in this age-group, or whether they are simply more likely to be reported by teachers, either because of the greater age and size of the pupils concerned or because of the relative lack of alternative special education facilities for older pupils. Here too longitudinal research is of some help.

In a follow-up of the original Isle of Wight study, Rutter et al.

(1976) found a slight increase in the rate of psychiatric disorder in early adolescence compared with four years earlier, when the pupils were ten. More important, they did not report any significant increase in the number of children with 'conduct disorders', or overt behaviour problems of an outwardly disruptive type.

The potential usefulness of early intervention can be considered in two ways. It is reasonable to suppose that the outlook is better if help, of whatever form, is offered at an early stage, before the behaviour has become well established. This is well documented in the case of school refusal (Hersov 1977), though there appears to be remarkably little systematic evidence with respect to disruptive behaviour.

Advocating intervention at an early stage in the development of disruptive behaviour, however, is quite different from advocating that treatment and support services should concentrate on the primary school or early secondary school age-groups in order to prevent the more seriously disruptive problems of the later secondary school years. To do so would make sense only if it were possible to predict reliably which pupils would be presenting problems towards the end of their school careers. It is by no means clear that this is possible. Although, as noted already, the rate of psychiatric disorder in early adolescence was marginally higher than in ten-year-olds, just over half the adolescents had started to present problems *in adolescence*. Just under half were young people whose problems had persisted from childhood. This hardly supports the view that disruptive behaviour can be prevented by a heavy concentration of resources on the younger age-groups.

Special education and support services: a paradox?

Special schools
Prior to the 1944 Education Act, it was difficult for LEAs to make special educational provision for their disruptive and/or emotionally disturbed pupils, even when they wished to do so. A handful of pioneer child guidance clinics had received financial support in the 1930s, and Section 80 of the 1921 Education Act empowered authorities to cater for children's health and physical education. This somewhat vague wording provided a loophole through which a few education departments were able to pay the fees for difficult pupils to attend voluntary homes or schools.

The public first became more widely aware of difficult and disturbing pupils during the Second World War following evacuation of children from inner-city areas. Galloway and Goodwin (1979) drew a slightly cynical comparison between the Second World War and the Boer War. In the latter, the discovery that only one in three possible recruits was physically fit enough for active service hastened a decision to do something about the health of the nation's children. In the Second World War, the discovery that many inner-city children could not, or would not, conform to the expectations and requirements of families on whom they were billeted hastened a decision to provide statutory recognition of the needs of difficult and disturbing pupils.

The ministerial regulations issued after the 1944 Education Act (Ministry of Education 1945) placed a *duty* on LEAs to provide special education for maladjusted children. Previously, they had merely been empowered to do so by the vague wording of Section 80 of the 1921 Education Act.

Yet the obligation was less clear than it sounded. As we have already seen, maladjustment is essentially an administrative concept, used primarily to provide special education. Hence, it can be argued that the Act's requirement that LEAs provide special education for maladjusted pupils is largely meaningless. It was, and still is, theoretically possible for a school medical officer formally to ascertain a child as maladjusted by signing the form prescribed by the 1944 Act. In practice, this form was seldom signed unless there was a good chance of special education being made available.

In other words, identification as maladjusted depended less on the child and the difficulties he presented than on the availability of special educational facilities. This point was well recognised by the Warnock Committee (DES 1978), who pointed out that in 1977, one London borough ascertained as maladjusted ten times more children than another. Earlier, DES (1966) statistics had reported that only 3.4 pupils per 20,000 in the northern region were being educated, or awaiting placement, in special schools or classes for the maladjusted, compared with 28.3 in the Metropolitan area. While northerners may naturally like to consider themselves better adjusted than southerners, the differences do seem to reflect differences in the provision of facilities rather than in the incidence of maladjustment.

For all its weaknesses, though, the 1944 Education Act provided the first statutory acknowledgement that some disruptive pupils might, in certain circumstances, have special educational needs which were not being met by the pastoral and disciplinary system in their ordinary schools. Expansion in special school or special class places for maladjusted pupils was rapid. In 1950 only 587 children were receiving full-time education in special schools or classes for the maladjusted. By 1976 the number had risen to 17,653 (DES 1976). The only other category of handicap recognised under the 1944 Act which showed comparable expansion was that of educationally subnormal pupils (from 15,173 full-time pupils in 1950, to 53,772 in 1976).

It is worth noting that educational subnormality and maladjustment are the only two of ten categories currently recognised under the Act in which the handicap is defined in educational and psychological terms. All the others are defined primarily on medical, or at least physical, grounds. This, however, raises an important point about the concept of handicap, namely that children do not fall neatly into administrative categories. The Warnock Report was absolutely clear about this; indeed one of its principal recommendations was that new legislation should be introduced to abolish the existing categories. The committee agreed that the emphasis in the assessment of handicapped children should change from allocation to categories, to description of educational needs.

This is consistent with the recommendations of DES Circular 2/75 to all LEAs in 1975 which gave greater prominence to the child's current educational needs, and suggested that educational psychologists, rather than school medical officers, should be responsible 'for conveying to the authority a recommendation about the nature of the special education required and where it should be provided'. The circular also recommended that formal ascertainment should only be carried out in the rare cases where a LEA wished to enforce special education against a parent's wishes. By making the whole process more informal, it would become possible to use special education facilities more flexibly, with greater possibilities of return to the mainstream. It would also reduce the artificial, and often arbitrary, distinction between maladjusted pupils and other pupils who presented behavioural problems without being labelled maladjusted.

These developments have an important implication for policy towards disruptive pupils. If a pupil is formally ascertained as maladjusted under provision in the 1944 Education Act, the LEA *must* place him in a special school or class recognised by the DES as providing education appropriate to the age, ability and aptitude of maladjusted pupils. When formal ascertainment became virtually a thing of the past, following recommendations to LEAs in Circular 2/75, it became easier for LEAs to use special schools to cater for a wider range of pupils presenting difficult behaviour. Indirectly, this led to LEAs discovering a need for a wider range of facilities outside the established special school system. This had theoretically always been possible. The 1944 Act was in fact quite clear both that formal ascertainment was not universally necessary, and that a recognised special school or special class would be unnecessary or inappropriate for many pupils with milder forms of handicap. In practice, however, the formality of ascertainment procedures helped to focus public and professional attention on the small number of supposedly 'maladjusted' pupils, rather than on the much larger number of pupils who disrupted their classes.

Recent developments

As argued above, the special education system has catered for a minority of disruptive pupils – normally in full-time schools for the maladjusted. The majority have always remained in their ordinary schools, either with or without attention from the educational support services. These services are described more fully in Chapter 4. At this stage we need only note that they have expanded as rapidly as the number of special school places.

In 1955, for example, only 140 educational psychologists were employed by LEAs in England and Wales (Williams 1974). By 1970 the number was over 900. This was based roughly on the Summerfield Report's recommended ratio of 1 educational psychologist to 10,000 pupils *of school age* (DES 1968). In a moment of optimism, or idealism, the Warnock Committee advocated a threefold expansion, by calling for a ratio of 1 educational psychologist per 6,000 of the population *aged 0–19*. Economic circumstances in the UK in the 1980s will ensure that this remains a recommendation. Yet even without further expansion, the profession's growth since the 1944 Education Act has been remarkable. Similar growth has occurred in the number of social workers with responsibility for children, child psychiatrists and education welfare officers.

Recent developments need to be seen against this background of increased educational expenditure on special schools and the support services. They also need to be seen in the light of the rather obvious fact that neither special schools nor the support services can reasonably be expected to solve the problem of disruptive behaviour in schools. We need only recall evidence from the recent major surveys that between 5 and 20 per cent of pupils, depending on the area surveyed and the procedures used in the survey, show marked behavioural problems at any one time. Problem behaviour is not confined to the minority who can be referred to outside 'experts'. The most important recent developments have been outside the special school system, and have acknowledged the existence of disruptive pupils more explicitly than was possible with the vague, quasi-medical concept of maladjustment.

Recognising that many LEAs were starting to make specific provisions for disruptive pupils outside the established special school system, the Inspectorate carried out a survey of 'behavioural units' (HMI 1978). The results showed that 72 per cent of 96 LEAs in England had established special units for problem pupils. The majority of these served more than one school, but because of possible misunderstanding in the wording of the initial inquiry to LEAs, it was not clear how many schools had established their own units, but were not included in the survey because the unit was not regarded as a formal LEA initiative.

The fact that schools are starting to establish provision for disruptive pupils on their own initiative is one of the reasons why reliable information on the development of units for disruptive pupils appears almost impossible to obtain. As we shall see in Chapter 4 however, there is considerable evidence that units set up by individual schools, for pupils at these schools, have developed in parallel with units set up by LEAs to cater for pupils from a large number of schools.

Conclusions

Disruptive behaviour may be attracting more attention than ever before, but that is quite different from saying that more pupils are disruptive than ever before, or that the problems they present are more intransigent than ever before. Yet teachers feel they are expected to achieve better and better results, with fewer and fewer resources, in a more and more complex world. We are suggesting that disruptive pupils are a predictable, even healthy, focus for anxiety which is only partly of their own making.

Our argument is that disruptive pupils must be seen in a broader educational context as only one of many challenges facing teachers. This must not, however, be taken to imply any lack of recognition of the severity of the problems they present, nor of the time and energy which teachers spend in dealing with them.

The research reported in this chapter provides no more than a background against which to examine aspects of the problem in more detail. The research is not discouraging. In spite of the large number of pupils reported by teachers as presenting notable problems, the evidence does not suggest that schools today are any closer to anarchy than they were in the 1920s and 1930s. Even more encouraging, there is evidence from the major surveys that schools can themselves influence the behaviour of their pupils. We return to this question in Chapter 4.

The research reported so far nevertheless contains one important omission, namely information about the small minority of pupils whose behaviour is so severely disruptive that their teachers no longer feel able to tolerate their presence in the schools. These pupils deserve a chapter to themselves.

Chapter 2

The last resort – exclusion and suspension from school

The legal and administrative position

Demanding that a pupil be removed from school, either temporarily or permanently, is the ultimate sanction available to teachers. From time to time every secondary school head-teacher must give careful thought to this possibility. For reasons we discuss later, primary school heads find themselves at the end of the road less often than their secondary school colleagues. Unfortunately the terms exclusion, suspension and expulsion are not always used in the same way. They imply different actions in different LEAs. As the terms themselves become blurred, so does their legal and administrative underpinning. What follows is an attempt to clarify that confusion.

Procedures for removing a pupil from school vary from LEA to LEA. As neither the 1944 nor subsequent Education Acts provide guidance, they are based partly on case law and partly on informal agreement between the LEA and its teachers. Informal agreement is necessary for two reasons. First, case law does not provide a sufficiently comprehensive formula to cover all eventualities. Second, problems resulting in a child's removal from school arouse strong feelings, both in parents, teachers and the pupil himself. Resolving these problems requires flexibility. Too rigid a legal framework might reduce the chances of a mutually acceptable compromise being worked out. A confrontation in which each side stands by his legal rights can hardly provide a suitable climate for such a compromise.

The head-teacher's right to suspend pupils is not in dispute. On this issue, most LEA Articles of Government for secondary schools make clear that the head is responsible for the school's internal organisation, management and discipline. He is also expected to exercise supervision over teaching and non-teaching staff. He has the power to suspend pupils from attendance for any reason that he considers adequate, but must report the case to the chairman of the governing or managing body. The parents must be told that they have the right of appeal to the governors or managers, and the facts must be reported to the chief education officer. In specifying these or similar arrangements in their Articles of Government, LEAs are merely using the rather broad powers conferred on them by the 1944 Education Act.

Unfortunately, these guidelines raise as many questions as they answer. They make the *procedure* clear, but do not explain what suspension *means*. For example, is it restricted to cases where the head sees no immediate prospect of readmitting the pupil, or does it also include short-term exclusion from school? Similarly, no mention is made of ways in which suspension can end, nor of the LEA's responsibility in the matter. What tends to happen is that LEAs make their own arrangements, generally influenced by the limited amount of available case law. In the case of *Spiers* v. *Warrington Corporation* (1954), the judge established a definition of exclusion and suspension. These definitions are used in the descriptions which follow.

Expulsion

Although theoretically possible in law, few LEAs allow head-teachers to expel pupils. The reason lies mainly in a legal technicality. Expelling a pupil implies that his name is removed from the school register. Under Section 36 of the 1944 Education Act, parents are required to ensure that their child receives education appropriate to his 'age, ability and aptitude'. In practice, most parents meet this requirement by registering him at a school in their LEA. Having registered him, they have a legal obligation to ensure that he attends. The LEA, for its part, must provide a school at which the child may be registered.

Removing his name from the register creates serious administrative problems. Strictly speaking, some short-term alternatives to full-time education are possible only when a child is a registered pupil. If he is not, he cannot, in principle, be offered home tuition, nor can he be placed in a special centre for disruptive pupils or poor attenders which is outside the special school system. The rationale is simply that these forms of provision are intended to be temporary. If there is no school to which the child can return, he cannot logically be offered a temporary alternative.

Suspension

The principal characteristic of suspension is that the head-teacher sees no immediate possibility of readmitting the pupil. In practice this can mean that he will not be prepared to admit him under any circumstances. Suspension is thus the functional equivalent of expulsion, except that the pupil remains on the school roll, with the consequent theoretical possibility of readmission. Suspension is principally intended to cover two sorts of problem. The first covers incidents of quite exceptional severity, such as an assault on a teacher, in which the pupil's indefinite removal is considered necessary for the general good. In the second case, suspension is the culmination of a series of problems. The precipitating incident may not be too serious in itself, but is viewed against a background of long-term intransigence.

Head-teachers are expected to inform the chief education officer of all cases of suspension. They are also expected to inform the parents in writing of their right of appeal to the school governors. If the governors uphold the head-teacher's action, the parents in theory also have a right of appeal to the Education Committee and to the DES. In practice, appeals against suspension are extremely rare. The reason is that an appeal to the governors is likely to be a distressing experience for the parents, and has very little chance of success. This, rather than any desire to avoid embarrassing the school, is why most LEA employees, such as education officers or educational psychologists, try to dissuade parents from appealing.

There are three reasons why an appeal is likely to be distressing to parents and is almost certainly doomed to failure. The first is that parents of suspended pupils are seldom as articulate as teachers. Hence, they are less skilled in putting their case persuasively. Most, though not all, boards of governors would probably allow a parent to bring a friend to the appeal meeting, but parents seldom request this. In any case, many parents would be unable to afford the legal advice which would be necessary for them to present a case effectively. The second reason is that the parents were not present when their child's misbehaviour occurred, and hence cannot easily challenge the teachers' version. Moreover, problems which result in suspension arouse strong feelings in teachers. The head-teacher will be able to call a succession of teachers, each of whom will describe a long list of misdemeanours. The third reason why an appeal is likely to fail is that most governing bodies see their job as supporting the head-teacher. Governors who are interested in their school's reputation and standards will naturally wish to support the head-teacher in upholding law and order.

There appear to be no national figures on the number of appeals following suspension. In Sheffield there were only four or five in the four-year period 1975–79. None of these were successful. Nor is it known how often parents appeal to the Education Committee or the DES. In Sheffield this did not happen at all in the four-year period.

The LEA's obligation in cases of suspension seems clear. If the parents appeal, it must ensure that the appeal is heard. If the head-teacher's action is upheld, or if no appeal is made, the LEA must offer the parents alternative education. Before deciding what can be offered, the authority will probably obtain specialist advice, usually from its educational psychology service. Possible forms of alternative education which can be offered will be dealt with later in this chapter.

Exclusion

In most LEAs the head-teacher may temporarily exclude a pupil in order to maintain the smooth running of the school. Pupils may also be excluded for medical reasons, including infestation, but these lie beyond the scope of this book. Following exclusion the child must be kept at home pending discussion between the head-teacher and the child's parents. It is expected that these discussions will take place in the near future, and will be followed by the child's return to school.

Exclusion is intended to cater for severe problems in which the child's temporary removal from school is desirable either for his own safety, or for that of other pupils or staff, or to restore the stability of the school community. Examples are a violent clash between two pupils, in which neither will back down, or a particularly severe act of vandalism towards school property. In such cases, exclusion can act as a 'cooling-off period', giving both pupils and teachers a chance to see the problem in a wider perspective.

Exclusion can also be used to cater for less severe problems, in which the head-teacher considers it necessary to enlist the parents' more active cooperation. Such cases normally involve a clear refusal to accept the teacher's authority in some way. The pupil will be re-admitted when he agrees to accept the school's authority in future, and his parents agree to support the school. Three examples are consistent refusal to do any work for a particular teacher, refusal to accept punishment and failure to wear the current school uniform.

It is important to be clear that exclusion is not generally regarded by the LEA as a punishment. Nor is any appeal possible against exclusion. In each case the rationale is the same. The aim of exclusion is not to deprive the child of his education, but to enlist parental cooperation in order to educate him more successfully. It is hoped that parents will make immediate contact with the head-teacher, so that the matter can be speedily resolved. Unfortunately this does not always happen.

It follows that no time-limit can be placed on exclusion, since to do so would formally deny the child his right to education. This would be of questionable legality, since provision of alternative education only becomes a matter for the LEA in cases of suspension. What can happen, however, is that the head-teacher may feel a week's 'cooling-off period' is needed. When parents ring up to arrange an appointment, they may find that the head-teacher is sorry, but the first appointment he can offer is in a week's time, owing to previous appointments. The distinction between setting a time-limit of one week, and setting no time-limit, but being unable to arrange an appointment with parents within the next seven days to discuss conditions for their child's return, sounds – and is – a legalistic nicety. Not surprisingly, it is often more readily appreciated by administrators than by teachers. However, legalistic nicety or not, it does illustrate the complex administrative issues involved in exclusion.

Another characteristic of exclusion is that the child is technically absent from school illegally if his absence lasts more than a day or two. To see the reason for this, we must understand the teacher's legal position *in loco parentis*. Teachers, like parents, are expected to impose reasonable rules and regulations to ensure their pupils' health and safety. Like parents, they are also empowered to impose punishment, including corporal punishment. If a parent supports a pupil in refusing to accept the school's rules and regulations, or in refusing to accept punishment, she is considered to be acting unreasonably. More specifically, by not cooperating with the teachers in the execution of their duties *in loco parentis*, she is unlawfully withholding her child from school.

For example, a not uncommon reason for exclusion is refusal to accept corporal punishment. Whatever views a parent may have about corporal punishment, she can be prosecuted under Section 40 of the 1944 Education Act if she does not insist on her child returning to school and accepting the punishment (Newell 1979). In theory a change of school is a way out of the impasse. Unfortunately this is not always possible, either because no other local school has vacancies or, more frequently, because no other school is willing to admit a pupil whose parents wish to deny teachers the right to use whatever punishment they consider necessary. This probably provides as good an example as any of the LEA's paramount need for tact and flexibility in dealing with cases of exclusion.

The LEA's obligations in cases of exclusion are less clear than in cases of suspension. As exclusion is strictly a matter between the school, the parents and pupil, with the school willing to accept the pupil's return provided reasonable cooperation is forthcoming, there is no obvious reason why the governors or the chief education officer need be informed. The DES has issued no guidance on the matter. It is clear not only that policy varies widely between LEAs but also that practice can vary widely within LEAs (Grunsell 1979).

Comment

It is not difficult to criticise the procedures involved in excluding and suspending pupils from school. By taking a dry, legalistic point of view, the cards can appear hopelessly stacked against parents and child. In cases of suspension the right of appeal offers no safeguards; it is naïve to expect the governors of the suspending school to be sufficiently unbiased to act as arbiters – even if parents could be sufficiently informed about the facts to argue their case. In the case of exclusion, one can sympathise with a parent who sincerely believes the problem lies as much in the school as in her child, yet knows that she may create further problems by failing to cooperate with the school against what she believes – however mistakenly – to be her child's interests.

Yet this legalistic viewpoint is only valid to a limited degree. The system described here *can* be abused – but so can any system which is not so rigid that further problems inevitably arise from its lack of flexibility. Exclusion and suspension result from a human interaction. Dealing with problems arising from exclusion and suspension requires tact, sensitiveness and often compromise. It is the head-teacher's responsibility to inform a parent of her child's exclusion in such a way that the ground is prepared for a meeting to arrange for his return. Equally, it is the head's responsibility to try to ensure that this meeting takes place in a mutually cooperative spirit. The LEA has two responsibilities. The first is to keep a watching brief on the use of exclusion. If it is used with undue frequency, or if letters to parents seem likely to close rather than open the door to the child's successful return to school, then these matters can be raised with the head-teacher concerned. The LEA's second responsibility is to provide specialist support services when needed to assist in the process of successful return.

In cases of suspension the head must inform parents that their child will not be readmitted in the foreseeable future, and that the question of his future education must be decided by the chief education officer. Giving this information in such a way that the parents are not antagonised against the whole education system is not easy.

The number of children involved

Problems in obtaining reliable figures
Like most LEAs, the DES has been reluctant to obtain figures on the number of excluded pupils. There are reasons for this reluctance.

Disruptive pupils have become a politically sensitive issue. Collecting, let alone publishing, details about them could give the topic greater attention from educationists than it deserves. Pressure groups, varying from politicians of both major parties to some teachers' organisations, would certainly give it undue attention. One can sympathise with those who feel that the spotlight of publicity can only cloud the issue. Rational decisions are seldom made when people's views are polarised. There is nevertheless a very real danger in this view. Few administrators welcome public discussion, let alone public accountability. Yet if the issues are not discussed, there is a serious risk of decisions being based on administrative expediency rather than educational need.

Another difficulty in obtaining reliable figures arises in defining the precise circumstances in which exclusion merges into suspension. In theory the position is quite straightforward, as we saw earlier but in practice, confusion frequently arises. Only the three most common sources of confusion need to be mentioned.

1. Following exclusion, head-teachers quite often request special schooling, and refuse readmission until the request has been considered. By the time the LEA has decided to accept the request, readmission is inappropriate, either because a special school place will shortly be offered, or because the head now takes the view that acceptance of his request implies that the child ought not to be in an ordinary school. These pupils are then, in practice, suspended.
2. Children with a history of troublesome behaviour are frequently offered a change of school, even if their behaviour has not resulted in exclusion. If the trial at the new school fails, the original school is sometimes unwilling to readmit the child. Strictly, these should be regarded as cases of suspension from the original school.
3. Following exclusion, it occasionally becomes obvious that the child will not be readmitted, even though the parents do not defy the school's authority in any specific way. This is most likely to occur when a meeting with parents and child leaves the head-teacher with a feeling that no useful purpose will be served by readmission. This should be regarded as suspension. It contrasts with cases when the head-teacher remains willing to readmit as soon as the parents and student agree to accept his authority, for example regarding homework or wearing school uniform. These are clearly exclusions.

This analysis of the 'grey area' between exclusion and suspension illustrates a practical difficulty in collecting reliable figures. It also illustrates two other points. First, every case needs careful investigation in its own right. Reliable figures simply cannot be collected by administrative decree. Second, something which starts as an exclusion can easily escalate into suspension unless handled with great sensitivity. Heavy-handed or over-enthusiastic intervention by officers of the LEA may tip the delicate balance between exclusion and the more serious problem of suspension.

It will be appreciated that collecting reliable figures on exclusion and suspension is undoubtedly difficult and time-consuming. Moreover, real dangers can arise from the exercise. From a policy point of view, reliable figures are nevertheless important. At local level, the LEA needs to know both how many pupils are suspended from school, and whether satisfactory alternative education can be provided for them. Without this information the LEA cannot reach an informed decision on the allocation of resources – for example whether to open a special unit for disruptive pupils, or to concentrate on providing a more effective support system for schools. At national level, the DES needs reliable information in order to advise LEAs about the size and nature of the problem in the country as a whole, and the policy options open to them.

Local studies

York et al. (1972) reported that 31 pupils were suspended from Edinburgh schools in the two years 1967–69, representing roughly 0.023 per cent of the total on roll. They also studied a further 10 pupils who were suspended before these dates. Information about the children and their families will be given in Chapter 3. The most common reasons for suspension in York's study were attacks on other children, usually described as 'vicious', and intolerable temper outbursts or aggressive, disruptive and uncooperative behaviour.

An interesting observation was that over twice as many children were suspended in the winter months, when opportunities for outdoor play were restricted. The mean age at the time of suspension was twelve, with a range from five to fifteen. The peak ages were the year before leaving primary school for boys and, for boys and girls, the penultimate year of compulsory education. Just under one-third of the children were attending special schools. Special school pupils were thirty times more likely to be suspended than pupils from ordinary schools. Of the 41 pupils, roughly 83 per cent were boys, far exceeding the usual excess of boys reported as deviant by teachers in epidemiological studies (Rutter et al. 1970, 1975a). At follow-up, between one and three years after suspension, only 4 of the 25 children still at school were both living at home and attending ordinary schools. None, however, were causing particular concern in the approved school, special school or psychiatric unit to which they had been transferred.

The prevalence of suspension in Sheffield was reported in a small-scale study by Galloway (1976a). He noted that 34 pupils had been suspended or excluded for at least a week in the twelve months from May 1973–74. When allowance was made for the raising of the school age to sixteen in 1972, and the fact that his data contained temporary exclusions in addition to indefinite suspensions, the overall prevalence of suspension seemed similar to that reported in Edinburgh by York and his colleagues. Galloway was, however, able to obtain some information about the pupils' schools. Neither large schools nor schools in the most socially disadvantaged areas were more likely to suspend pupils than small schools in more privileged areas. On the other hand, comprehensive schools which had incorporated a selective school on secondary reorganisation did seem more likely to suspend than those which had not.

The difficulty in obtaining reliable information is well illustrated by Grunsell (1979). He studied the figures from an anonymous LEA, Baxbridge. In 1975 and 1976 the number of pupils indefinitely suspended in Baxbridge was 42 and 40 respectively. 'In November 1976,' Grunsell notes

> an instruction was issued to schools that in future the procedure for
> notifying suspensions was to be strictly observed. In 1977 the
> permanent suspensions rose to 63 and temporary suspensions
> doubled. Clearly, at least some of the apparent increase can be
> explained as evidence only of more accurate reporting by schools.
> Heightened awareness, both inside and out, of disruptive
> behaviour and the use of exclusion must lead to some increase in
> the reporting of exclusions which have previously been dealt with
> informally by the schools.

Grunsell concludes bluntly that 'there is no objective consistency in what the figures measure'.

Support for this argument came from his observation that three of the fourteen comprehensive schools in Baxbridge accounted for 45 per cent of all suspensions, and five for 60 per cent. The pupils most at risk of suspension were in their final two years of compulsory education, and of West Indian origin. Over half the permanent suspensions in 1977 were of West Indian origin, although the West Indian population in the borough as a whole was only 10–12 per cent. Earlier Coard (1971) had drawn attention to the disproportionate number of West Indian pupils in special schools for moderately educationally subnormal (ESN (M)) children. Moreover, Rutter et al. (1976) had reported higher rates of 'deviance' in West Indian pupils as reported by teachers on a behaviour questionnaire (Rutter 1967). Grunsell's evidence suggests that the possibility of West Indian pupils being overrepresented in other forms of special education, besides schools for ESN (M) pupils, should be taken seriously.

The studies of Grunsell and of York et al. (1972) highlight the problems in obtaining information about exclusion and suspension. The results can be virtually impossible to interpret, even if the figures themselves appear to demonstrate an obvious trend. Subtle changes in a LEA's policy on reporting exclusions may lead to major changes in head-teachers' willingness to use this sanction. Similarly neither York et al. nor Galloway (1976a) gave adequate background information on the procedures schools were expected to follow in notifying the chief education officer of suspensions, nor of the precise criteria which were used in defining them.

For these reasons it is hard to tell whether their figures reflect a true picture, or merely constitute the tip of the iceberg. It is theoretically possible, for example, that the five schools in Grunsell's study which accounted for 60 per cent of all suspensions might simply have been more conscientious in reporting suspensions. In an attempt to obtain a clearer picture, exclusions and suspensions were recorded for four years in an LEA which had already established a well-defined set of procedures for reporting them.

Exclusion and suspension from schools in Sheffield

Local education authority policy on reporting exclusion or suspension
Recognising teachers' concern about disruptive behaviour, in 1974 the chief education officer set up a weekly meeting under the chairmanship of a senior assistant education officer. The meeting was attended by a senior member of the LEA's psychological service and education social work service (known elsewhere as the education welfare service). It had four principal functions. The first was to act as a clearing house for all information about excluded or suspended pupils. The second was to request and coordinate inquiries about the children concerned, with particular emphasis on their future educational needs. The third was to make arrangements for their future education, and the fourth to consider the adequacy of existing resources for them.

Head-teachers were notified, both in writing and at meetings, of the distinction between exclusion and suspension. They were advised, as a matter of enlightened self-interest, to follow strictly the procedures for reporting suspensions and for notifying parents in writing of their right of appeal. They were also requested to inform the office about all temporary exclusions.

Accuracy of information received

For three reasons, a high level of confidence can be placed in the view that information received by the weekly meeting constituted a valid picture of exclusion and suspension in the city's schools. The first reason was that the meeting was a weekly one, with frequent feedback to head-teachers from the senior assistant education officer (AEO) or his representative. Second, and perhaps most important, the senior AEO had established extremely good informal relationships with secondary school head-teachers, both as a body and individually. They all knew of the weekly meeting, and most of them recognised it as a constructive attempt by the administration and support services to resolve problems resulting from severely disruptive behaviour. Third, the LEA's policy was well known to members of the psychological service and education social work service. Members of both services spent a lot of their time in schools, and were seriously concerned about the problems of pupils out of school. An efficient grape-vine ensured that the weekly meeting heard about most of the children whose exclusion or suspension had not been reported formally. It is worth mentioning, however, that the overwhelming majority came through the normal channels.

Sheffield's system could be regarded as a model for other LEAs. It ensures that the LEA is aware of virtually all exclusions and suspensions, and hence is in a position to carry out necessary inquiries. These can take the form of discussion with the excluding school, or of specialist investigation into the needs of the child and his family.

In one sense, however, the Sheffield model may inflate the number of excluded or suspended pupils. The mere fact of setting up a formal system may encourage teachers to use it. As we saw in Chapter 1, Parkinson's law applies to disruptive pupils; the number of pupils thought to require special services increases in proportion to the availability of such services. Taking the analogy a stage further, the existence of formal channels may discourage some head-teachers both from making further attempts to cater for the pupil themselves, and from negotiating a transfer informally with a colleague in a neighbouring school. On the other hand, the Sheffield model generally prevents suspended pupils becoming 'lost' in the system, and enables decisions on a possible change of school to be made in the light of evidence from a variety of sources. This is not to say that children never get 'lost' in the system in Sheffield. We did hear of three or four children who were out of school for a prolonged period of time without the LEA appearing to know or take action about them. We cannot *prove* there were not many more of these children – it is never possible to prove a negative – but we think it unlikely.

The one area in which the weekly meeting did not obtain reliable information was short-term exclusions. Head-teachers did not always report problems which were resolved rapidly. A frequent example at a small number of schools was exclusion for not wearing correct uniform. In such cases the student would be sent home, and told to return properly dressed. The LEA would only hear of such cases if absence was prolonged by more than a few days. Similarly, some head-teachers would only report exclusions after the event, when it became clear that they could not negotiate an immediate return to school with the parents. In practice, there was reasonable confidence that virtually all exclusions lasting more than one or two weeks were reported. For research purposes, however, no exclusion was recorded which did not last at least three weeks. This reduced still further the margin of error, and ensured that the results related to students who had presented severe problems, at least in the administrative sense. One further problem was that the weekly meeting only dealt with exclusions and suspensions from ordinary schools. Those from special schools were dealt with through a separate administrative channel. Brief details were nevertheless obtained from the heads of special schools. This information was necessary, as York et al. (1972) had reported a disproportionate number of suspensions from special education.

The number of pupils

Table 2.1 shows the number of pupils suspended or excluded for at least three weeks in each of the four years of the study. It would be easy to sensationalise these figures, but unjustified. They show that the number of suspended pupils increased by a third between 1975–76 and 1976–77, and that the number of excluded and suspended pupils combined nearly doubled between 1975–76 and 1977–78.

Table 2.1
Pupils suspended from schools in Sheffield LEA or excluded for at least three weeks from 1975–1979*

	1975–76	1976–77	1977–78	1978–79	Total
Number suspended	26	39	46	38	149
Number excluded for at least 3 weeks	22	29	48	29	128
Total	48	68	94	67	277*

* Including eleven pupils known to have been suspended or excluded from special schools, but about whom no further information was available.

Before making any hasty conclusions about the deteriorating fabric of society, it is as well to consider two points. The weekly meeting had been held for well over a year by the start of the 1975–76 school year, but the procedures were only just starting to become well known and recognised throughout the LEA. Moreover, the chief education officer's request that head-teachers report exclusions in addition to suspensions was not made until May 1975. It is therefore quite possible that the increase in 1976–77 and 1977–78 reflected greater awareness of the LEA's procedures, with a consequent willingness to use them.

The second point is that Sheffield's school population at the time was around 105,000. We are therefore considering a very small proportion of pupils indeed. There was no year in which the number of excluded and suspended pupils from primary schools exceeded 0.01 per cent (1 per 10,000 on roll). The peak age for secondary school pupils was the final year of compulsory education, except in 1977–78 when more fourth-year pupils were reported. Even in secondary schools, though, there was no age-group in which the number of pupils reported exceeded 0.38 per cent of the total on roll for that year.

The importance of this is that a relatively small increase in absolute numbers can seem like a dramatic increase if viewed in terms of proportions. Spread out across the LEA, the increase between 1975–6 and 1977–78 represented a theoretical average increase of just over one pupil excluded or suspended from each secondrary school. What it actually indicated, as we shall see shortly, is a sharp increase in a small number of schools. The figures provide no evidence for a city-wide epidemic of disruptive behaviour.

One further point about Table 2.1 is that our project started in January 1978. The project itself may therefore have affected the number of exclusions or suspensions. We cannot, of course, be certain about this. Subjectively, we thought that one or two schools might be resorting to exclusion more readily than in the past, 'to show them what the problem is'. Conversely, we thought one school might be more reluctant to exclude. Again, we cannot prove a negative, but we do not think the project affected the figures in any important way. The existence of the project certainly cannot explain the increase in 1977–78 and the drop in 1978–79.

The pupils' age and sex are shown in Table 2.2. For ease of reading, exclusions and suspensions have been combined, as have results from the four years of the survey. It is seen that exclusion or suspension from primary schools was very rare indeed, and occurred on average less than once a year for girls. In secondary schools, there

Table 2.2
Age and sex of pupils suspended from Sheffield schools, or excluded for at least three weeks, 1975–79

Age	Number excluded or suspended		
	Boys	Girls	Total
Primary (5–11)	16	2	18
Secondary (12 and 13)	12	10	22
(14)	19	21	40
(15)	49	31	80
(16)	80	26	106
Total	176	90	266

was a steady age-related increase, the only exception being that more girls were reported in their penultimate year of compulsory education than in their final year. The sharpest increases were between fourteen- and fifteen-year-old boys and between fifteen- and sixteen-year-old boys. In this respect exclusion and suspension follow a slightly different pattern to persistent unauthorised absence from school where the sharpest increase is between fifteen- and sixteen-year-olds for boys and girls (Galloway 1976a, 1980a).

Reasons for exclusion and suspension
As indicated earlier in the chapter, both exclusion and suspension could result from a single incident of exceptional severity. More often, though, they reflected a gradual build-up of tension to a level which the head-teacher was not prepared to accept. The incidents which precipitated exclusion or suspension are nevertheless of some interest and are shown in Table 2.3. Again, the picture which emerges is not one of any radical breakdown into anarchy. Over four years only 12 out of 266 exclusions or suspensions were precipitated by an act of violence towards a teacher.

The categories were formulated from head-teachers' letters to the chief education officer, reporting that they had excluded or suspended a pupil. In reading the categories, and the reports from which they were derived, one is struck by the generality of the incident which prompted the head-teacher's action. There was seldom evidence of uncontrollable behaviour; much more often, the head's letter reflected a gradual escalation to the point of no return. Most letters emphasised the student's previous bad behaviour. Many emphasised the pre-

Table 2.3
Precipitating incidents resulting in suspension from Sheffield schools, or exclusion for at least three weeks, 1975–79

	Number of pupils	Per cent
Abuse/insolence to teachers	48	18.0
Unspecified bad behaviour	42	15.8
Refusal to accept discipline/disobedience	33	12.4
Bullying/violence to other pupils	29	10.9
Persistent absence	23	8.7
Refusal to accept punishment	20	7.5
Breaking school rules	18	6.8
Disrupting lessons	17	6.4
Violence towards teacher	12	4.5
Bad influence on other pupils	11	4.1
'Socio-medical', e.g. infestation, scabies, etc.	5	1.9
Theft/vandalism	5	1.9
Acts outside school	3	1.1
Total	266	100

vious warnings he had received. It was tempting to wonder whether some pupils felt bemused that on this occasion, after so many 'last warnings', they really were being suspended.

A possibility suggested by York et al. (1972) was that exclusion and suspension might be more common in the winter months. The Sheffield inquiry showed a mild but reasonably consistent trend for more students to be reported in November, February and March than in other months. Over the four years 40 per cent of the pupils were excluded or suspended in these months. October and January together accounted for a further 20 per cent. The evidence suggests that disruptive behaviour resulting in exclusion is most likely in the winter months. It is particularly likely in the middle of the term, when the previous holiday has been forgotten, and the next one is not yet in sight.

Outcome
A student's exclusion had already lasted three weeks before he was included in the survey. Almost by definition, this meant that arrang-

ing a return to school was proving extremely difficult. Suspended pupils had frequently been seen by members of the LEA's psychological or education social work services before their suspension, but this seldom meant that alternative education could be arranged quickly. In practice, 71 per cent of pupils in our survey had either returned to their original school or were receiving some alternative form of education within eight weeks of their exclusion or suspension.

Table 2.4 shows the outcomes for the 266 pupils, in order of frequency. Almost all the 71 pupils who returned to their original school had been excluded. It is worth remembering, though, that Table 2.1 shows 128 pupils as excluded. Hence, it was apparently considered impossible or impractical to readmit a substantial minority of pupils whose exclusion was in theory regarded as temporary. The 49 pupils who reached school-leaving age before any alternative education could be offered were almost all in their final year of compulsory education when they were excluded or suspended. Placing such pupils presents three related difficulties.

First, no head-teacher will welcome a final-year pupil with a history of seriously disruptive behaviour at another school. Apart from any

Table 2.4

Outcome following suspension from Sheffield schools, or exclusion for at least three weeks, 1975–79

	Number of pupils	Per cent
Readmitted	71	26.7
Over school-leaving age before alternative education offered	49	18.4
Transferred to another school	43	16.2
Referred to home tuition service	34	12.8
Transferred to a special school	28	10.5
Placed in centre for disruptive pupils	17	6.4
Placed in care	14	5.3
Readmitted pending transfer to another school	4	1.5
Referred to another LEA	3	1.1
Placed in centre for poor attenders	2	0.7
Not known	1	0.4
Total	266	100

other considerations, each school runs its own integrated course for students in their final two years, leading to the Certificate of Secondary Education (CSE). A lot of CSE work is based on internal assessment, which creates obstacles for a student who enters the school more than half-way through the course, in the middle of his final year. Second, special school places are not generally available to fifth-year pupils, though students whose suspension occurs at the beginning of the year, in September or October, may be offered a place in the LEA's centre for disruptive adolescents. Third, students excluded or suspended towards the end of their school careers are themselves not always desperately eager to make a fresh start at school. Except in a small minority of cases, the choice lay between referring final-year pupils to the LEA's home tuition service, which was not always able to help as physically ill children were, quite reasonably, given priority, and simply waiting for them to reach the legal school-leaving age. In several cases parents asked for permission for the student to seek employment, since the LEA was not able to offer them education. In such cases the LEA could only regret that lack of flexibility in the law prevented this. Anyone employing a school-age pupil is breaking the law.

It is of some interest that only 6 per cent of excluded or suspended pupils were placed in the LEA's centre for disruptive adolescents. This centre catered for up to twenty pupils, mostly in their final year of compulsory schooling. The reason for so few students in the survey being referred was straightforward. The majority of pupils admitted to the centre were admitted because exclusion or suspension were imminent, rather than because either had actually occurred. Transfer to another ordinary school and, especially for pupils aged fourteen or less, transfer to a special school were both much more frequent outcomes than transfer to a special centre. The evidence from Sheffield shows that such centres cannot sensibly be expected to cater for more than a small minority of severely disruptive pupils.

The school's contribution

We have concentrated so far on the students themselves rather than their schools. In view of public and professional concern about disruptive pupils, this seems reasonable. Focusing the investigation on the students without also considering their schools is nevertheless one-sided. Two questions need answering at this stage:

(a) Are excluded and suspended pupils distributed evenly between the LEA's secondary schools (overlooking for the moment the small number of primary and special school pupils involved)?

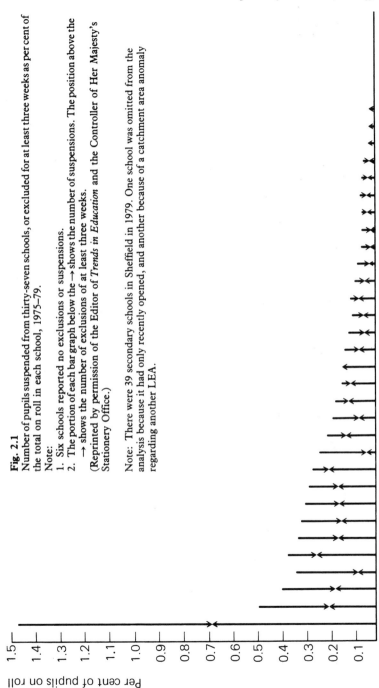

Fig. 2.1
Number of pupils suspended from thirty-seven schools, or excluded for at least three weeks as per cent of the total on roll in each school, 1975–79.

Note:
1. Six schools reported no exclusions or suspensions.
2. The portion of each bar graph below the → shows the number of suspensions. The position above the → shows the number of exclusions of at least three weeks.

(Reprinted by permission of the Editor of *Trends in Education* and the Controller of Her Majesty's Stationery Office.)

Note: There were 39 secondary schools in Sheffield in 1979. One school was omitted from the analysis because it had only recently opened, and another because of a catchment area anomaly regarding another LEA.

(b) If not, do they come from schools with a common set of problems in their catchment areas?

Figure 2.1 shows the proportion of excluded and suspended pupils at thirty-seven of the city's secondary schools, as a per cent of the total on roll at each school. On each bar graph, the portion below the arrow represents the number of suspensions, and the portion above the arrow the number of exclusions. In this figure, the four school years 1975–79 have been combined. However, the differences between schools were consistent from year to year. They did not result from one exceptional year. Bar graphs cannot be shown for six schools, since these schools reported no exclusions or suspensions in the four-year period.

Figure 2.1 shows massive differences between schools in the use of exclusion and suspension. In general, there was a fairly close relationship between the two sanctions – schools which used one tended also to use the other. Exceptions were the fourth and eleventh schools from the left which suspended a fairly small proportion of students, but excluded a relatively high proportion.

The next question was whether a head-teacher's decision to exclude or suspend could be predicted from information about a school's catchment area. In other words, did some districts in the city produce an exceptional number of students who could not be contained in school? Using data from the 1971 Census we were able to construct a profile of each school's catchment area, with details such as parental occupation, quality of housing, size of family and so on. We also obtained details about the curriculum in each school, about the organisation of pastoral care and remedial teaching and about structural aspects of the school, such as its size and the age and number of buildings. The statistical technique of multiple regression was then used to investigate the relationship between all these variables and exclusion and suspension.

The results are described in more detail elsewhere (Galloway et al. 1981a). All that needs to be said here is that we found no obvious relationship between a school's use of exclusion or suspension and any aspect of its catchment area. It was not the case, for example, that schools with the most socially disadvantaged pupils tended to exclude or suspend most pupils. In this respect, exclusion differed strikingly from persistent unauthorised absence. If you know the number of a school's pupils who are authorised to receive free meals because of low parental income, you can predict the number of persistent absentees with a high level of reliability (Galloway 1976a, 1980a). No such readily identifiable relationships exist in the case of exclusion and suspension.

Comment

One of the reasons for establishing formal procedures for reporting exclusion and suspension was concern about pupils who remained without education for prolonged periods following 'unofficial' exclusion. Predictably, though, setting up a weekly meeting to deal with the problem did not solve it. The number of pupils who remained without education for over eight weeks illustrates this. The weekly meeting may in fact have increased the number of exclusions and suspensions. As we have already argued, the number of problem children increases to exceed the availability of services for them. Bureaucratising procedures may legitimise them. The alternative, though, is ignorance. The LEA has an obligation both to its teachers and to its pupils. It cannot afford to remain ignorant of the fate of its least successful or most troublesome pupils. A more reasonable question is whether an increase in the use of exclusion occurred in all schools or only in schools with high exclusion or suspension rates in the first place.

In his pilot project, Galloway (1976a) reported only thirty-four pupils suspended or excluded for at least one week in the twelve months from May 1973–74. There is strong evidence that this figure was a considerable underestimate, owing to incomplete reporting at a time when the LEA was still establishing its procedures. More important, though, the schools which reported most suspensions or exclusions in 1973–74 were mainly the same schools which reported most in the four years 1975–79. Schools which reported few or none in 1973–74 also reported few or none in 1975–79. (In a minority of schools substantial changes were observed; they generally coincided with a change of head-teacher or deputy head.) The evidence implies that the increase in excluded and suspended pupils was due largely to an increase at a small number of schools.

It is perhaps worth repeating here that exclusion and suspension represent only one small part of the problem of disruptive behaviour. They constitute the tip of the iceberg, in the sense that most disruptive behaviour is dealt with internally, never coming to the notice of authorities outside the school. They nevertheless merit careful consideration. Exclusion or suspension can have a far-reaching effect on the pupil and on his family. The amount of time spent on these pupils by teachers and by senior members of the LEA is out of all proportion to their numbers. Just as important, they raise questions both about the nature of disruptive behaviour in school, and about the school's contribution to standards of behaviour.

The Sheffield survey demonstrated enormous differences between schools in their use of exclusion and suspension, which could not be explained by differences in the pupils' backgrounds. Continuing the iceberg analogy, do schools with the highest rates of exclusion and suspension also have the highest rates of disruptive behaviour? Alternative possibilities are: (a) that some schools use these sanctions much more readily than others; (b) that some schools are much more flexible or tolerant in their reactions to disruptive behaviour than others. These possibilities are dealt with in Chapters 6 and 7, as part of a more wide-ranging description of policy and practice in schools selected for more intensive study.

The heavy preponderance of secondary school pupils in the survey also raises questions about the nature of disruptive behaviour. Primary school children may, for example, simply be easier than adolescents to contain when they present difficult behaviour. The epidemiological literature reviewed in Chapter 1 provided only limited evidence that disruptive behaviour becomes more common in older pupils. A different explanation, though, is that special school places are more readily available to primary school pupils. Sheffield is generously supplied with special schools, particularly schools for maladjusted pupils. The evidence suggests that difficult primary school children are labelled maladjusted and placed in a special school, while difficult secondary school children are, in extreme cases, labelled disruptive and excluded or suspended.

Special schools in Sheffield do nevertheless seem to cater for disruptive pupils, as was seen in Table 2.4. Moreover, special school pupils constituted a small minority of those in the survey. In this respect, the Sheffield results differ markedly from the Edinburgh survey. York et al. (1972) point out that Edinburgh's day schools for the maladjusted and the mentally handicapped had only female teaching staff. They suggest this as one reason why special schools might have difficulty in channelling the aggressive behaviour of older pupils. In Sheffield, special schools had male and female teachers, though obviously one cannot draw any conclusions about their lower exclusion rates from this fact.

Conclusions

The uneven distribution between schools in the Sheffield survey is consistent with Grunsell's (1979) observation in 'Baxbridge'. It suggests strongly that the causes of exclusion or suspension, if not of disruptive behaviour, lie in the attitudes, policies and practices of the school. This implies the need for a sociological orientation when investigating disruptive behaviour, with an emphasis on the social influences which the school exerts on the individual. On the other hand, teachers, psychologists and psychiatrists emphasise disturbed or deviant characteristics in the pupils themselves, or in their families. This implies the need for a psychological orientation with the emphasis on the way individual or family psychopathology affects adjustment to school or to society.

The results presented so far from the Sheffield surveys do not demonstrate that some schools have exceptionally high levels of disruptive behaviour, though that remains a distinct possibility. What they do imply is that a pupil's chances of being excluded or suspended are influenced at least as much, and probably more, by which school he happens to attend, as by any stress in his family or any constitutional factors in the pupil himself. Yet an interest in the pupils' schools cannot justify us in overlooking the pupils and their families. In Chapter 3 we describe some of the pupils who most disturb their teachers.

Disruptive pupils and their families

Introduction

In Chapter 1 we noted that teachers report far more children as showing quite severe behaviour problems and/or learning difficulties than can sensibly be referred to the support services. In Chapter 2 we noted that severely disruptive behaviour resulting in exclusion or suspension occurs far more frequently in some schools than in others. We now need to ask what sort of pupils are being described in these surveys.

This question can be tackled from several angles. First, teachers' descriptions of their behaviour must be examined; after all, the problems they present are, by definition, problems for teachers. The most severely disruptive pupils are often referred to psychologists or psychiatrists for assessment or treatment, so we also need to know whether specialist assessment throws any light on their behaviour. Similarly, family circumstances need investigating, to see whether the problems presented in school can reasonably be viewed as a reaction to stress at home. Finally, but by no means least, we must try to look at disruptive behaviour from the student's perspective. This requires an assessment of his educational strengths and weaknesses, since these may be related to his social adjustment at school. Equally important, though, it involves listening to his side of the story.

Overview from large-scale surveys

As noted in Chapter 1, many child psychiatrists and psychologists distinguish between 'conduct' disorders and 'neurotic' disorders. The former include aggressive, acting-out, delinquent, overt disruptive behaviour. The latter refer to emotional problems, such as withdrawn or anxious behaviour, timidity, nervousness and so on, which undoubtedly create distress for the child and his close family but do not generally involve open conflict with authority. A surprising but fairly consistent feature of the research is that the overlap between problems reported by parents and by teachers is low.

This is a common source of friction between teachers and parents. When a child presents problems at school, his parents not infrequently deny that they have similar difficulties with him at home. The teachers may then feel that the parents are being uncooperative, 'covering up' for the child. On the other hand, when parents seek advice from teachers about their child's disturbing behaviour at home, they may be told that he is no problem at school. In such a circumstance the teacher may consider the home problem is caused by the parents. Superficially, the explanation for the apparently small overlap is straightforward. Teachers tend to report overtly difficult behaviour, while parents appear more sensitive to the so-called 'neurotic' disorders (Rutter et al. 1970). This explanation, though, only begs further questions.

With a class of around thirty pupils, it is not difficult to understand why teachers should overlook withdrawn or anxious pupils who pose no threat to classroom order. Equally, it is easy to see why they should be quick to recognise more overtly disruptive forms of behaviour. What is much less obvious, and more interesting, is why these overtly disruptive forms of behaviour should occur more often at school than at home – since it is hardly reasonable to argue that they would remain unnoticed at home if they occurred regularly. Superficially, answers can be found easily enough by contrasting the need for order and discipline at school with the lack of discipline in some homes. If a child is never expected to sit still, he cannot be called disruptive for failing to do so. Teachers and parents certainly differ in what they regard as 'good' behaviour. Just as important, teachers differ between themselves in what they consider appropriate. At one school, rules on uniform are strictly enforced; at another, school uniform has been abandoned. At one school, all pupils are called by their surnames; at another, no pupil is called by his surname. The influence of school rules and teachers' attitudes on pupils' behaviour is only gradually becoming recognised.

We have already seen that deviant behaviour reported by teachers was more common in London than on the Isle of Wight (Rutter et al. 1975a). The higher London rate applied to both boys and girls, though a larger proportion of London girls seemed to have problems which were confined to the home. With the London pupils there were some interesting ethnic differences. Children of Caribbean origin did not differ from white children in the prevalence of 'neurotic' or 'mixed' disorders. On the other hand Rutter's (1967) behaviour questionnaire for teachers showed that 'conduct' disorders were much more common in children of Caribbean origin. A further difference emerged from a comparison between West Indian and white girls. With the latter, emotional problems were more common than more overt behaviour difficulties. In West Indian girls, in contrast, as in West Indian boys, the more overt problems were much more common (Rutter et al. 1975b).

As noted in Chapter 2, Grunsell (1979) found West Indian pupils more likely to be suspended from school than non-immigrants, and Coard (1971) had highlighted their overrepresentation in special schools for the ESN(M). In order to interpret these results we need to know something about their family circumstances. Rutter et al. (1975c) showed that West Indian pupils tended to attend schools with less satisfactory conditions. They also pointed out that the West Indian children were more likely to live in unsatisfactory housing, that their fathers were more likely to be in unskilled or semi-skilled occupations and that they were more likely to have had unsatisfactory experiences early in life. All of these observations could contribute both to the behaviour reported by teachers, and to their generally lower educational attainments (Yule et al. 1975). A further possibility is that unconscious bias and expectations of teachers might contribute to underachievement.

Research on the family backgrounds of disruptive pupils is complicated by difficulty in interpreting what the results mean. On commonsense grounds one could expect a parent's mental or physical illness to affect the child's emotional stability. There is, in fact, evidence that this is the case (Rutter 1966). On the Isle of Wight, psychiatric disorder in the mother was strongly associated with psychiatric disorder in the child. This was not, however, the case in London (Rutter et al. 1975b). The reason seemed to be in the much higher rate of psychiatric problems, mainly depression, in the mothers of 'normal' London children. The important point is that the severity of stress imposed on the child by family problems varies from area to area. Another way of looking at this is to assume that the same event may constitute much more of a problem, both for parent and for child, in some areas than in others.

The parents separating provides another illustration of this point. Children from broken homes in London were more likely to be diagnosed as showing psychiatric disorder than Isle of Wight children from broken homes. The explanation seemed to be in the fact that the Isle of Wight parents were much more likely to have married again, happily in most cases. In other words, the break-up of their parents' marriage perhaps constituted more long-lasting stress for the London children, and this was subsequently reflected in their behaviour at home and at school.

The surveys we have considered in this chapter and in Chapter 1 investigated *all* children born in a given area. The results illustrated broad tendencies. They could not, and were never intended to, discover causal factors in particular cases. A mother's poor psychiatric health illustrates the distinction. Her symptoms were less likely to be associated with psychiatric disorder in her children in London than on the Isle of Wight. Yet that evidence could not justify a London teacher or psychologist in concluding that any particular child was unaffected by his mother's illness.

The exceptional minority

Introduction
Surveys based on complete populations illustrate the prevalence of certain problems. They also identify the potential stresses which often accompany these problems. At best they illustrate the factors in the pupil himself, and his family, and as we see in Chapter 4, in his school, which might repay attention when investigating the reasons for a pupil's difficult behaviour. They do not remove the need for careful investigation in individual cases. A further, and perhaps obvious limitation is that the surveys we have discussed so far provide only the broadest overview of disruptive behaviour. This is necessary, since many teachers would argue that greater stress is caused by frequent petty acts of indiscipline from several pupils than from a single severe act by one or two pupils. The most severely disruptive minority nevertheless repay detailed study.

Constitutional factors
Several researchers have investigated the possibility of a link between violent or other severely disruptive behaviour and atypical 'autonomic' functioning. It is assumed that erratic, exceptionally deviant behaviour is partly caused by, or at least associated with, physical factors. These may arise either from constitutional handicap originating at or before birth, or from stress in early childhood (Laycock 1968; Hare 1970).

For teachers, belief in a physical basis to disruptive behaviour is encouraging in the short term but intensely depressing in the longer term. In the short term, the results may provide a superficial explanation to behaviour which has for long been causing anxiety. Yet as parents of so-called dyslexic children know to their cost, diagnoses and treatment are two quite different things. Some parents feel relieved when their child is diagnosed dyslexic, mistaking the label for an explanation of his reading difficulty. Similarly, both teachers and parents may feel relieved if specialist investigation discovers some medical or consitutional abnormality in a disturbing child. Yet they remain no nearer finding a solution to the problem.

There is in fact evidence that disruptive pupils differ from 'normal' pupils in their reactions to certain stimuli. Davies and Maliphant (1974), for example, showed that disruptive boys in a residential school were significantly slower to learn from punishment than their control group of pupils whose teachers were unworried about their behaviour. An interesting point about Davies and Maliphant's experiment was that it took place in a school for 'ordinary' pupils. In a laboratory experiment adolescent boys were given brief mild electric shocks in a task which required them to over-compensate for the effects of a well-known visual illusion. The disruptive individuals received significantly more shocks than a control group. 'Punishment' led to a reduction in their errors, but the effects seemed relatively short-lived. The authors comment that 'this seemed analogous to their typical response to punishment or disciplinary procedures in everyday life.'

A somewhat different line of inquiry has investigated the connection between atypical brainwave patterns and aggressive behaviour. It is certainly the case that children with some neurological problems are more susceptible to aggressive or disruptive behaviour. As part of the Isle of Wight study, Graham and Rutter (1968b) found some evidence of behaviour disturbance in 34 per cent of epileptic children. They also found that children with lesions above the brainstem were significantly more likely to show signs of behaviour disturbance in the classroom than children whose lesion lay below the brainstem. In a study of physically handicapped children integrated into ordinary classes, Anderson (1973) found that the only group which displayed more behaviour problems than their able-bodied peers was that with neurological abnormalities.

It is one thing to demonstrate an association between certain forms of neuropathology and disruptive behaviour. It is quite another to conclude that *any* disruptive child is likely to require neurological assessment. A great deal of professional time and energy has been spent investigating a possible connection between aggressive outbursts and temporal lobe epilepsy. Harris (1978) points out that it is not rare for some children with a record of aggressive outbursts to be referred for electroencephalography (an EEG) in a search for temporal lobe abnormality, even though the child has never been seen to have a seizure.

The research evidence is far from conclusive, however. Harris quotes a detailed review by Kligman and Goldberg (1975). They concluded that methodological problems prevented any firm decision about the existence of an association between some forms of aggressive behaviour and temporal lobe epilepsy. Moreover, even if such an association *could* be demonstrated, it would still be impossible to draw any direct link between the epilepsy and the aggressive behaviour. The reason was that social and other physiological variables could also contribute to the association.

Harris' own conclusion is that no consistent relationship exists between specific symptoms and EEG abnormalities. The high incidence of abnormal EEG findings in children, particularly children with behaviour disorders, is at least partly due to the inclusion of children known to be epileptic or brain-damaged. As we have seen, these children *are* known to be particularly prone to behaviour problems.

The best that may be said of research on the association between disruptive behaviour and physical factors is that the latter may contribute to the problems of some children, but do not cause them. Only behaviour which is so grossly abnormal that education in an ordinary school would never be considered could meaningfully be said to be caused by constitutional factors. Children with diagnosed epilepsy or some other forms of brain damage illustrate the argument. These children are undeniably more likely to present their parents or their teachers with problems. Yet they are by no means certain to do so. Whether they actually behave disruptively will depend on other social, educational and medical factors. Perhaps the best way to conceptualise the evidence is that in some cases constitutional factors lower the threshold at which the child starts to behave in an erratic or disturbing way.

Surveys of suspended pupils

The survey of pupils suspended from Edinburgh schools for disruptive behaviour was mentioned in the review of exclusion and suspension in Chapter 2 (York et al. 1972). It provides a comprehensive clinical picture of these pupils. As a group the children were dull, compared with the general population in Scotland at the time. Only one pupil obtained an IQ of 110 or over, and 65 per cent had scores of less than 90. Their educational attainments were correspondingly low. Nearly two-thirds were at least two and a half years retarded in reading, and only 16 per cent obtained a reading age commensurate with their chronological age.

The authors reported none of the suspended children as displaying behaviour which was mainly neurotic in nature. Psychiatric records were available on 34 with conduct disorder the primary diagnosis for half the children. A further 7 showed what the authors called 'mixed behaviour disorder', including both 'conduct' and 'neurotic' characteristics. The remaining 10 children were described as suffering from either mental subnormality, hyperkinetic syndrome, depressive illness or childhood psychosis. As a group they were said to be 'extraordinarily delinquent and aggressive'.

The pupils were generally in good health when interviewed, but nearly 25 per cent had a medical history implying possible cerebral dysfunction. A few of the parents suffered from severe physical illness, but psychiatric disorder was much more common. Just over 80 per cent of suspended children were found to have at least one parent with psychiatric disorder or evidence of personality disturbance. In three-quarters of families with both parents living together, there was friction between the parents.

The Edinburgh study focused on psychiatric assessment of the children and their families. A different approach was used in a small-scale study of suspended pupils by Longworth-Dames (1977). He used a high school personality questionnaire (Cattell and Cattell 1975) to compare the personality characteristics of eight suspended pupils with normal controls selected from the same class in school. Perhaps surprisingly, he found no significant differences. The suspended pupils seemed as stable as their peers who had not been in trouble with authority at school. The suspended pupils did obtain significantly higher scores on the Bristol Social Adjustment Guide (Stott 1963). This was to be expected, though, since the guides were completed by teachers who would hardly be expected to have charitable feelings towards pupils they had suspended from attendance.

Having found no differences in personality between suspended pupils and controls, Longworth-Dames suggested that the suspended group might 'be behaving in a very socially precise way, to maintain their image in their sub-culture'. In other words, they might be emotionally stable, well-adjusted individuals who had adopted a different value system to that of the school. Having identified themselves as a group, with an 'anti-school' identity, these pupils were under pressure to maintain their disruptive behaviour in order to maintain this identity. Thus, the teacher's disapproval was necessary in order to retain approval from the peer group.

This theme is developed further in Chapter 4. Here we need only observe that it exemplifies the distinction between sociological and psychological approaches to disruptive behaviour which we first noted in the Introduction. Longworth-Dames' sociological model emphasised the possible influence of the peer group in a pupil's relationship with authority. The psychological approach of York and his colleagues emphasised disorders in the pupils and their families. Yet their respective conclusions may have reflected their methodology more than differences in the pupils they studied, although Longworth-Dames' pupils were a good deal older than most of York's. The Edinburgh team did not report personality test scores. On the other hand, it is reasonable to assume that fuller details about Longworth-Dames' pupils, their history of conflict with their schools or with the police, and their family circumstances, might have given a child psychiatric team more than enough evidence on which to diagnose psychiatric disorder.

A study of pupils suspended from Sheffield schools

Purpose
The research on severely disruptive pupils contains a number of apparent anomalies. Apart from the different emphasis placed on psychiatric ill-health by York et al. (1972) and Longworth-Dames (1977), the uneven distribution between secondary schools and the preponderance of older pupils in the Sheffield surveys both raised interesting questions about the needs of suspended pupils – and of their schools.

The LEA had two reasons for an interest in the subject. The most pressing one resulted from the chief education officer's obligation to offer alternative education following suspension. Do suspended pupils have special educational needs, or can it safely be assumed that the majority should be able to fit into another ordinary secondary school? The fact of suspension suggests the former, while the fact that many schools seldom, if ever, resorted to suspension might suggest the latter for at least some pupils. In the longer term, a clearer understanding of the background events leading up to suspension might help the LEA decide whether or not 'high-suspension' schools had exceptional disciplinary problems, and if so what additional forms of support would be helpful. We therefore decided to carry out a detailed study of pupils suspended from school.

Selection of pupils
We originally selected two samples. The first consisted of all pupils who were formally suspended from school between 1 May 1978 and 30 April 1979. The second consisted of pupils excluded in the same period who were still out of school, with no immediate prospect of return, four weeks after their exclusion. In practice, most of these

turned out to be *de facto* suspensions, using the term to include doubtful cases as explained in Chapter 2. The two original samples were therefore combined.

Altogether 58 pupils met the criterion of suspension or long-term exclusion, 15 girls and 43 boys. Of the 53 secondary-age pupils, 27 came from five schools. This, of course, is consistent with the earlier evidence on exclusion and suspension over four years. Only one pupil in the sample had been suspended from a special school. Information was sought from parents, from the pupils themselves and from their head-teachers. The parents of 6 children declined to take part in the study. In addition 5 were in the residential care of the local authority at the time of their suspension, and a sixth was placed in care shortly afterwards. It was possible to interview these children and their head-teachers, but not their parents. This meant that the parents of 45 suspended pupils were interviewed.

Information from parents

The purpose of the interview was to seek information about a range of social, psychological and educational factors that might have contributed to breakdown at school. As would be expected from the survey on exclusion and suspension over four years, it was clear that suspended pupils were not confined to the most disadvantaged areas of the city. While 51 per cent of the pupils lived in the older, less satisfactory forms of council accommodation, nearly 30 per cent owned their own homes.

It was noticeable, though, that just over a third had been at their current address for a year or less. The move did not always involve a change of school, but in several cases it necessitated a rather long journey to and from school. Few parents saw the move as a factor in their child's problems with the school. The change of house could nevertheless have contributed, in the same way that any other major upheaval can contribute to tension in quite different contexts.

In this respect, as in the varied quality of their housing, the families of suspended pupils differed strikingly from the families of persistent absentees, most of whom had been living for many years in substandard accommodation (Galloway 1980a). We wondered whether suspended pupils all came from the most disadvantaged parts of their school's catchment area. Although the schools varied widely in the districts they served, it might still be the case that most suspended pupils came from the most disadvantaged families in the school. Preliminary analysis indicated considerable variation from school to school in this respect. In some schools it certainly appeared to be the case; in others it did not.

The parents of 40 per cent of suspended pupils were separated or divorced, but very few families had been separated by the death of one partner. In both respects suspended students differed little from the comparison group of good attenders in a study of persistent absentees from a depressed part of Sheffield (Galloway et al. 1978; Galloway 1980a). Separation or divorce in 40 per cent of families seems a high rate, but on its own cannot be considered a causal factor. Neither parent was employed in 22 per cent of the families, though nearly twice this number had received social security or similar benefits within the previous twelve months. Just over half the mothers were working, in most cases part-time.

As a group the children seemed in good health when interviewed; only 16 per cent were reported to suffer from any chronic illness, such as bronchitis or repeated ear infections. In marked contrast, however, 69 per cent had a history of serious illnesses or accidents which had required in-patient treatment. In 27 per cent of cases there was a possibility of neurological impairment as a result of the illness or accident. Examples were meningitis in infancy with associated convulsions, and serious head injury following road accidents. The suspended pupils appeared much more prone to serious accidents or illnesses than their siblings.

It is virtually impossible to distinguish between cause and effects in such cases. The suspended pupils might have suffered accidents or illness *because* they were already vulnerable on temperamental or constitutional grounds. On the other hand, the accident or illness might have created heightened vulnerability to disordered behaviour, thus increasing the likelihood of it. From an educational point of view the distinction is not important. Whatever the reason, medical histories reported by parents suggest strongly that the pupils might constitute an exceptionally vulnerable group for temperamental or constitutional reasons.

Poor health was also a fairly frequent characteristic of the pupils' parents. Just under half the mothers reported some form of chronic illness, though this was incapacitating in very few cases. Turning to mental health, 44 per cent had either received medication for minor psychiatric symptoms such as depression or anxiety states, or reported symptoms associated with anxiety or depression. This conclusion was based on information provided in the course of the interviews and by a health questionnaire (Rutter et al. 1970) completed by the mother, or by the father in six cases where the mother was not present at the interview. In general the fathers appeared to enjoy better physical and mental health than the mothers. This is, of course, consistent with the results of epidemiological surveys of parents' health in urban areas.

43

Moreover, it should be remembered that well over a quarter of mothers of young children in a random sample drawn from a depressed inner-city area are likely to show some sort of handicapping psychiatric symptoms (Brown et al. 1975).

Schools were not alone in their concern about suspended pupils. Social-work agencies outside the education department had statutory or voluntary responsibility for 69 per cent of them. Nearly a quarter had been in care at some stage in their lives. In this respect, too, they differed from their siblings, since only 18 per cent had at least one sibling who had been in care. Here again the implication is that suspended pupils constituted an exceptionally vulnerable group.

The parents' reactions to their child's suspension varied widely. Perhaps understandably, nearly two-thirds said their initial reaction had been one of anger or resentment towards the school. By the time of the interview, however, 33 per cent said they now felt indifferent, even relieved by the event. A fairly common comment was: 'Well, at least he's out of school legally now.' This was said with particular feeling by a parent whose child was suspended a few days after she (the parent) had been fined £20 for the child's poor attendance.

Relationships between parents and school had been either strained or remarkably limited. A quarter of the parents said they had never met their child's teachers, though some admitted there had been indirect contact via an education welfare officer (EWO). The LEA clearly regarded suspension as a last resort. Thus, it was perhaps surprising that so many parents had never visited their child's school, especially as the EWO was almost always available to act as intermediary, if necessary providing transport.

More surprising still, in over half the cases the pupil was sent home with a letter informing his parents of the suspension, or told to tell his parents that a letter was in the post. The schools were therefore relying on pupils, who in most cases they regarded as unreliable, to give their parents news of their suspension. One boy and one girl (not siblings) did not return home that night, rather than face their parents, and three others did not give their parents the head-teacher's letter. One boy continued to leave home at the normal time in the morning, returning at the correct time in the evening. It was a week before his parents eventually had a showdown with him about his increasingly difficult behaviour at home, and discovered what had happened.

Most parents were nevertheless ready to say whether they experienced problems with the child at home. A parallel form of Rutter's behaviour questionnaire for teachers is designed for parents (Rutter et al. 1970). Like the teachers' scale, it was developed as a screening technique to identify children with possible psychiatric disorder. It contains several statements about behaviour, and about aspects of health which are often related to emotional stability. Parents of forty-two pupils completed the questionnaire. Just over 45 per cent of the pupils were given scores indicating likely disorder (i.e. above Rutter's criterion for investigating the child in more detail). Like the teachers' scale, the parents' questionnaire distinguishes between conduct, neurotic and mixed disorders. While 26 per cent of the sample were rated as showing behaviour which was primarily of the 'conduct disorder' type, the remaining 19 per cent showed mixed or neurotic disorders.

Delinquency

As a group the students were highly delinquent. Two-thirds of the boys and 87 per cent of the girls were known to the police for criminal acts. The high percentage of girls is surprising; in the general population, boys are far more likely to be in trouble than girls. These results may lend some indirect support to the subjective impression of many teachers and psychologists. While more boys present behavioural problems than girls, the most intransigent problems of all are presented by girls. We saw in Chapter 2 that fewer girls are suspended than boys. It is possible that teachers view delinquency in girls more seriously than in boys, thus increasing the likelihood of their suspension. Another possibility, though, is that chronically disruptive behaviour from girls is less likely to be confined to the school, and more likely to extend into the home and community.

Related to the delinquency findings, 78 per cent of parents stated that their child had truanted from school, at least occasionally. Truancy here meant that the parents were unaware of the absence, though several parents also admitted that they sometimes condoned absence from school when the child should theoretically have been attending. The high truancy rate is consistent with the view that truancy is just one aspect of a wider pattern of disruption and delinquent behaviour (Hersov 1960; Tyerman 1968; Galloway 1980a).

Educational background

Over two-thirds of the suspended pupils were extremely backward educationally, using a criterion of a reading age at least three years below their chronological age. They also tended to be of well below average intelligence. Each pupil was given a short form of the verbal scale of Wechsler's (1949) *Intelligence Scale for Children*. The mean IQ was 82, with a standard deviation of 13. This indicates that about 66 per cent of the sample obtained scores between 67 and 95. In fact, seven children obtained scores below 70, and none above 110.

The implication of these results, is, of course, that for a sizeable minority of pupils, successful return to the same or another ordinary school would be likely to impose considerable strain on the school's remedial teaching resources. To state the obvious, it is not helpful to return a potentially disruptive pupil to a situation in which educational failure is guaranteed, due to a mismatch between his own attainments and the school's curriculum.

There was some evidence, however, that this might happen owing to doubt regarding the causal relationship between disruptive behaviour and low scholastic attainments. The intelligence and reading test scores were obtained by David Galloway when interviewing the pupils. They suggested that the pupils as a group were of low verbal intelligence, and that many might experience some difficulty in coping with any curriculum that was not designed with the needs of slow learners in mind. In contrast, when head-teachers were asked for their view on each pupil's intelligence, they ranked only 37 per cent as 'below average' or 'very poor'. When asked about educational attainments, they placed 76 per cent in these categories. Thus, it seems possible that head-teachers were sometimes too ready to regard disruptive behaviour as the cause of low attainments, overestimating the pupil's own intellectual ability. One is reminded of the comment 'could do better', on end-of-term reports, and wonders how often it is accurate.

Surprisingly little information was available about the students' behaviour and attendance at primary school (or at infant school in the case of junior or middle school pupils). Records from the previous school gave no information on these subjects for over half the pupils. Poor attendance was noted on the records of only 11 per cent of pupils, and poor behaviour on only 21 per cent. By making the – admittedly dubious – assumption that exceptional problems would be noted on the LEA's record form which accompanies the pupil throughout his school career, it is possible to infer that the majority of suspended pupils had not presented severe problems at their previous schools.

Head-teachers frequently deplored the suspended pupils' choice of friends; 46 per cent were said to be a bad influence on others, but only 10 per cent were considered easily led. Perhaps this constituted an oblique compliment to their leadership qualities! A substantial minority (40%) were said to be 'out on a limb' socially, with few, if any, friends. Interviews with parents confirmed the general impression obtained from head-teachers that only a minority of the pupils were socially isolated. Nearly half the parents mentioned specific hobbies, or membership of a youth club or other youth organisation.

We wondered whether suspended pupils had clashed with male or female teachers exclusively. Slightly to our surprise, head-teachers said that 14 per cent had only presented problems with men, and the same proportion with women. The rest had not discriminated between the sexes. A variety of sanctions had been used prior to suspension. The most frequently noted were corporal punishment, reported by 72 per cent of the boys' head-teachers and 35 per cent of the girls', detention and some form of daily report system. With the latter, teachers would sign a form at the end of each lesson, making comments on the pupil's work and behaviour.

We asked head-teachers about their underlying aim in suspending each pupil. (We also asked about the incidents which precipitated suspension, but these are discussed below, with the pupil's own accounts.) The most common reported aim in suspending pupils was to maintain the safety of staff and/or other pupils. This was relevant in 39 per cent of the suspensions. Making a public demonstration to other pupils that certain behaviour would not be tolerated was mentioned by 31 per cent of heads. Nearly as many (29%) saw suspension as a way of making the Education Committee or the chief education officer provide some alternative form of education. While relationships between staff in the LEA's central administration and head-teachers were generally extremely good, a minority of heads clearly felt that formal suspension might be regarded as a crisis which would encourage the LEA to take action more rapidly. It is worth adding that this was seldom a correct assumption. The LEA's procedures, described in Chapter 2, placed as high priority on rapid investigation of pupils who were in danger of suspension, as on pupils who had actually been suspended.

The pupils' perspective
The importance teachers, sociologists and psychologists attach to pupils' accounts of their own disruptive behaviour depends on their philosophy. At one end of the spectrum is the view that pupils cannot be sufficiently objective to give any valid or meaningful account of their own experiences at school. This is well illustrated in a different context by Meighan (1978). He sought permission from head-teachers to ask pupils what they thought about the lessons of student teachers. The majority of heads agreed. The results showed that almost all pupils took the exercise seriously, making balanced, constructive, occasionally humorous comments which generally coincided with the independent observations of the college lecturer. One or two heads, however, refused permission for the research to take place, claiming among other things that the pupils lacked the objectivity and maturity

to make such judgements, and that the exercise might incite them to indiscipline.

At the other end of the spectrum is the view that only pupils' accounts of disruptive behaviour should be taken seriously. The argument is that teachers have a need to justify their action by painting the pupil in the worst possible colours. This view is as naïve and unfounded as the view that pupils' accounts should be discounted. Both are necessary. The significance of an event can vary from individual to individual, depending on his part in it. The fact that pupils and teachers may describe the same event in different ways does not mean that either description is false.

In reporting pupils' accounts of events leading up to suspension, we have aimed to give a balanced picture of the total sample. We have also tried to illustrate the pressures which operate on pupils as well as teachers, and to identify some of the common themes which emerge when the pupil's description is compared with the head-teacher's.

Only 26 per cent of pupils interviewed denied that they had frequently been in trouble at school before their suspension. The majority were able to give a reasonably detailed account of the events which led up to their suspension, but a few seemed genuinely perplexed as to the reason for it. The incidents varied very widely. Almost the only consistent theme was that they frequently escalated from a relatively small beginning. This point is well illustrated in the following account from a fourteen-year-old boy, Paul:

> The nurse sent for me, and . . . . she started on about why I don't wash regular. And I said: 'I do get washed,' and she pulled back my hair and said: 'Look at that neck – it hasn't been washed in about two weeks.' And she carries on about how I used to get washed and why don't I now, and then she says: 'I'm going to check up on you on Monday, and if you're still dirty you've had it!' And then I were walking out and I were muttering to myself, and she says I told her: 'balls!' She said she were going to have a word with the head and I said: 'What about it?' She just walked off, so I went back to my classroom and I get sent for to go and see the head. And, er, he got cane out and said he were going to cane me – and I said I'm not having it because I didn't say it. So he just wrote on a piece of paper and told me to go home . . . my mum and dad got a letter about five days later.

The head-teacher confirmed the gist of this story, making clear that he regarded neither the original abuse, nor his subsequent action as presenting particularly severe problems. He had decided to cane Paul for two reasons. First, the boy had been reported for muttering abuse in a half-audible voice before; second, abuse to the school nurse must be seen to be disapproved of. When Paul refused to accept corporal punishment, the head excluded him, thinking the matter would be speedily resolved with parental support. Paul's parents, however, chose to support their son and made clear that they saw little hope of further cooperation with the head-teacher. What started as a relatively minor incident between pupil and nurse escalated to involve the head, an educational welfare officer, an educational psychologist and a senior member of the LEA administration who eventually arranged a change of school.

A sense of injustice usually prompted the more overt acts of defiance. A sixteen-year-old boy described this incident:

We had Mr K for biology while we were in the Unit* and he used to start picking on us, so we told him what to do, and the last time we had him he got us expelled . . . we had him from three to four, and he started shouting at us, and he used to threaten us with the stick for anything. And this young kid comes down with message from deputy head, saying: 'You've got to let us out at quarter to four.' And he said: 'No, I'm not letting them out until half past four.' And Pete told him he'd got to go and see his probation officer, and he were picking on us, because there were these other two kids throwing rubbers at each other, and he weren't doing nothing about them. And Pete and me said: 'Right, we're going at four' – so we just packed us books and put them away and went. He were sat down and never moved out of his chair, and just says: 'Go and sit down; you're not going.' And we just went, so he goes: 'Right, I'm reporting you for disobedience.' And the next day we had to see the head-teacher, and he says: 'I'm expelling you from school for disobedience.'

The head-teacher's need to support his staff came through clearly in several pupils' accounts. A fifteen-year-old boy told the interviewer:

There were me and Andrew Williams, and I threw this paper jet and it landed next to the teacher and she said: 'The next person to throw one, I'll walk out of the lesson.' So Andrew threw one, and then she goes: 'Right, that's it; I'm walking out; I'm not teaching you any more.' And half an hour later she came back into the lesson, and someone goes: 'I thought you weren't teaching us any more!' And she goes: 'I'm not, until certain boys are out of this class, but I'm not deciding that – headmaster'll decide it'. And then headmaster came and he said: 'Who wants to not take part in this lesson?' And he goes: 'If you don't want to take part, we'll put you in a class by yourself, and you can learn Geography by

* See Chapter 7.

yourself.' And nobody put their hand up, and the teacher who'd walked out said: 'I'm not teaching until these certain boys are out of the class.' And the head-teacher says: 'Who is it?' And she goes: 'Williams and Smith.' And after he'd taken us out of the class he goes: 'I'm going to carry this on further, not just put you in another class.' And that were it – we were expelled or excluded.

A few children showed intense resentment towards school in general, or towards particular teachers. Anne, a fifteen-year-old girl in the care of the local authority, told us:

All it were, was I told the teacher to fuck off, and she took me down to the hippo, I mean Mrs D. . . . I didn't do it for nothing – I did it on purpose. I hated that school so much I wanted to get chucked out. . . . Earlier that day I got caught wagging a lesson in the toilet. Someone snitched on me, so I went: 'Get lost', so I had to see the head, so he says if there's any more trouble he'll have to exclude me so that made me even more determined.

The bravado which comes through in this and a few other accounts was not simply intended to impress the research worker. Anne's teachers confirmed the details. Yet if some pupils seemed anxious to show themselves in the worst possible light, others were implausible for different reasons. The 'messing about' in the following account contained the only really serious incident of violence in our sample of suspended pupils:

Me and this lad, we were just messing about, pushing each other about. And I accidentally smacked him on the nose, and it broke it. So he just went out of the class, and I put my stuff away, my folder and that, and went after him – not fighting because his nose were bleeding. And the form teacher come and took me to the head's office . . . and they asked me what happened and I told them, and they says: 'Go and get your stuff and go home.'

Several points can be made about the pupils' accounts of their own behaviour. The tendency for quite small acts of indiscipline to escalate into major disciplinary confrontations has already been mentioned. In such cases there was seldom any important inconsistency between the head-teacher's description and the pupil's, though each saw the chain of events in a somewhat different light. Two related points should also be made at this stage. The first is that events culminating in suspension often reflected an attitude towards 'trouble-makers' that was shared, in an odd way, by pupils and teachers alike. Subject teachers felt their authority threatened by indiscipline, and were supported by the head in a confrontation. Yet the pupils themselves were often caught up in the same process. They too were unable to lose face, either in their own eyes or in the eyes of their peers. The 'labelling' processes which result in some teachers and pupils adopting mutually inconsistent goals is discussed in more detail in the next chapter.

The second point concerns the pupils themselves. Many were reacting to great personal stress, as described earlier in the chapter. Suspension often seemed to result from combining deviant individual or family psychopathology with an educational climate which facilitated polarisation between 'them' and 'us'. With some pupils, mainly from schools with high suspension rates, the sociological processes seemed critical. With others, mainly from schools which seldom suspended a pupil, psychological factors seemed more important. There were few pupils for whom either explanation appeared adequate on its own.

By the time they were interviewed, nearly half the pupils claimed to be pleased that they had been suspended, or at least indifferent. A minority of 33 per cent expressed anxiety at the effect suspension would have on their future examination or employment prospects. Some typical comments follow:

'Well my brother got a job, so I should be able to . . . it just didn't bother me.' (15-year-old girl, whose brother had also been suspended.)

'I were in a way [worried]. I were thinking about what my social worker would say, what he would do about it – whether he'd take me back into care, or try and get me back into school.' (14-year-old boy excluded for refusal to accept punishment. The social worker told him to go back to school and accept it.)

'No regrets. I hate school – just since coming here; it were all right in the Juniors. Teachers – they think they own you – bossing you all the time and hitting you [In my] first year I got cane 14 times – 28 strokes. Only had it once in fifth year.' (15-year-old boy.)

'I think it were great, to tell you the truth.' (15-year-old boy.)

'I'm not worried about it, but it's going to affect my job if I can't go back. . . . I want to go back to Bridge – I knew the teachers already at Bridge School. It'd be like starting on a new life at one of them other schools you mentioned.' (15-year-old boy.)

Few pupils were undiscriminating in their attitude towards teachers. Only 17 per cent claimed to dislike all or most of the teachers in their school. The majority claimed, not unreasonably, to like some and dislike others. A notable feature, though, was the intense dislike and resentment which 32 per cent felt towards one particular individual. It sometimes seemed as though a long-standing personality clash between pupil and teachers was at the root of the problem.

'Mrs Jones, she's great. But she turned when she got with them two [deputy heads]. She turned funny. She just started shouting and that . . .! I used to get on great with Mr Turner (a deputy head), but he's got a right bad temper on him sometimes – if his hip's hurting him – he's got arthritis, you see. . . . He should learn to control his temper if he's a school teacher. Listen. I can control my temper if I've got all my nieces and nephews here and they're running round when I'm watching telly. He should be able to control his.' (15-year-old girl.)

'Most of [teachers] were all right. There were just one or two; they didn't like me and I didn't like them. . . . I was all right in lessons – it were just in breaks I got picked on, me and one or two others . . . somebody tried to set fire alarm off and I were nowhere near it. I went down to toilet and I walked past and this teacher had got some kids for it, like. And he grabbed me and tried to blame it on me, and he run up the corridor shouting: "I've caught Black, I've caught Black," as if I were a criminal or something like that.' (15-year-old boy.)

'I like most of the teachers at school. Mrs K, French, I just dislike her. Because other teachers are right strict. She isn't and I got bored.' (15-year-old boy.)

'Only one were best – me form tutor. I always used to behave in her class – I'd rather be in her class . . . the other teachers – don't like them. They always tried to blame me for things. Like, someone were throwing snowballs, and one went through the car window and hit Mr L. And he blamed me for it, and I weren't there!' (13-year-old boy.)

The pupils' attitudes towards their own behaviour varied. Some claimed that everything had been exaggerated. Others openly acknowledged their disruptive influence.

'I think I were about worst in school, to tell you the truth. The other lads in trouble – they were following me as much as me getting into trouble with them – know what I mean?' (15-year-old boy.)

'To me it were just kids' stuff, know what I mean? I weren't right serious, throwing bombs and that. . . . To me it weren't serious, but to a teacher it probably were.' (15-year-old boy.)

'It isn't really bad. Teachers might not think that, but they never see the others – they're just as bad.' (15-year-old boy.)

'I thought it were a bit of a fuss o'er nowt. I'm no angel, but I just did me best – and if my best isn't good enough, that's it, isn't it?' (15-year-old boy.)

'Some days I were good, some days I were really bad, some days in between. It just depends on what side I get out of bed . . . we

used to have a gang – there were three people in it – called the
Really Rottens. Once they accused me of pinching some keys –
kept on accusing me. In the end they found it was some workmen,
but they never apologised to me.' (11-year-old boy.)

In the course of the interview pupils were asked about their behaviour at home, and about their relationship with other members of
their family. Just as their comments about school should be seen as
contributory factors in the events culminating in their suspension, so
the same applies to their comments about home.

'She fusses too much. She's old-fashioned. She thinks it's 1910, but
it's not, it's 1978. . . . She's a right to fuss in a way: she brought us
up – but she overdoes it a bit.' (15-year-old boy living with elderly
aunt.)

'My mum says she hated the sight of me – and she said it in court
as well. . . . Every time I go to see her, she tells me to piss off
home . . . it were always me what got in trouble with police. Our
Dan didn't, and our Ben didn't either. If I argue with my mother
our Ben hits me, and if I argue with our Ben, Dad hits me. So I
can't win any way. I asked to see Miss O (an educational
psychologist) again, but the deputy head always said she was busy.'
(15-year-old boy.)

'Mum threatens me – says she won't get me a job. But she will –
she always does in the end. Says I'm in disgrace – she's disgusted
with me or summat.' (15-year-old boy.)

'Mum always favoured my brothers. She'd give them lunch, not
me. Would buy them things, even after she'd left, but not me.'
(14-year-old girl.)

'All our family went to India, and I was left here with my big
brother, and he used to go out. Didn't come in till one o'clock, and
I was left alone, and that's when I got wagging [truanting]
ideas . . . it used to be great. We used to beat up people and go out
and that.' (14-year-old boy.)

Comment

As we have argued already, students and teachers often see the same
event in a different light. So far, we have concentrated on the pupil's
perspective for two reasons. First, the term 'disruptive pupil' implies
that the pupil creates the problems, so it is important to know what
sort of pupil we are considering. Second, we shall be reporting
teachers' descriptions of problem behaviour later in the book, as part
of a wider discussion of discipline and pastoral care.

The Sheffield study obtained results that confirmed some of the
earlier observations by York et al. (1972) in Edinburgh. In Sheffield,

as in Edinburgh, suspended pupils appeared to be a peculiarly vulnerable group. This was reflected both in their medical histories and in the data on intelligence and reading ability. These results were noteworthy, as the Sheffield sample contained a higher proportion of fifteen- to sixteen-year-olds, with an uneven distribution between the city's schools. Longworth-Dames (1977) suggested that suspended pupils may be behaving in a very appropriate way within their own subgroup. The interviews with parents and pupils, however, suggested that this is not the whole story.

Some pupils, certainly, were identified by teachers, and had identified themselves – as trouble-makers. Their hostility focused on one particular teacher as often as on the school as a whole. Moreover, a majority appeared to be members of a peer group which was reasonably stable, at least by its own code. On the other hand, it was equally clear that conditions at home were in many cases highly stressful, and that the pupils themselves might have challenged their teacher's tolerance and skill even if this had not been the case.

Nevertheless, two obvious implications emerge clearly both from the intensive study of suspended pupils, and from the city-wide survey of exclusion and suspension over four years. First, the evidence suggests strongly that although some pupils may present severe educational and behavioural difficulties in any context, whether these difficulties result in exclusion or suspension depends in many cases on which school they happen to be attending. The second implication is that we need more information about the development of prolonged tension between teachers and a small minority of their pupils.

Conclusions

Neither pupils nor head-teachers gave the impression that suspension generally results from a single explosively dramatic incident. We are not talking about a minority of pupils who differ in some way from all other pupils. We are talking about pupils at one end of a continuum. At the other end – and perhaps almost as rare – is the model pupil, always reliable and conscientious. The major epidemiological studies reviewed in Chapter 1 describe the large number of pupils with quite severe learning problems and 'clinically significant' signs of behavioural disturbance. Most of these pupils are never referred to specialist services. They and their problems do not differ in kind from suspended pupils, only in degree. In this sense, suspension from school may be seen as representing the tip of the iceberg.

Yet although all schools contain potentially disruptive pupils, some are clearly more able and willing to contain them. It is, of course, possible that some schools only contain their difficult pupils at the expense of the conforming majority. If so, we should expect schools with low exclusion or suspension rates to achieve unsatisfactory exam results. This is by no means always the case. Having described the extent and nature of the problem, the next stage is to look at current procedures for assessing and dealing with disruptive pupils. The relevance of these procedures for teachers can then be considered in the light of information about the pupils and their schools. It may be that some procedures facilitate understanding about the nature of the problem, while others impede the search for practical solutions.

Chapter 4

Assessment and treatment: reality or mirage?

Overview

The most severely disruptive pupils are vulnerable by reason of constitutional, family and educational factors. Yet they are unevenly distributed between schools. Some schools seldom, if ever feel the need to use the sanctions of exclusion or suspension; other schools, serving similar catchment areas, use them frequently. The implication is that assessment should focus not only on the pupil and his family, but also on his school. In order to resolve the problem we need to know why it occurs. Knowledge of a school's policies and its teachers' attitudes is often as important in understanding disruptive behaviour as knowledge about family stress and intellectual weakness.

In this chapter we review the most widely available procedures for the assessment and treatment of disruptive pupils. We explain why their lack of success is predictable, and discuss recent evidence about the influence of school policy, organisation and climate on pupil behaviour. Finally, we relate this evidence to some encouraging theoretical and practical developments in the management of disruptive pupils, and look at the implications for future research.

Support and/or treatment services

The distinction between support services and treatment services is not always understood, either by teachers or by members of the services themselves. If the aim is to offer a treatment service, it follows that children should be referred who are most likely to benefit from the treatments the agency can offer. These are *not* necessarily the children whose behaviour is most disturbing to their teachers. In contrast, a support service will encourage referral of the most disturbing children. The aim is not to offer treatment but to help the teachers who must continue to deal with the problem themselves.

School attendance problems illustrate the distinction. School phobia has an excellent prognosis following individual treatment, especially if the child is pre-adolescent, is referred soon after the start of the problem and does not live in a family with serious social problems (Hersov 1977). Such children constitute a tiny minority of all unauthorised absentees. Many agencies prefer to help teachers and EWOs in working with the larger number of unauthorised absentees who have a poor prognosis for individual treatment (Galloway 1980b).

Possible sources of help within the local education authority
Local education authorities vary in the resources they allocate to their support services. Inevitably, this is reflected in the quality of service offered to schools. Sheffield, for example, has for several years worked on a ratio of 1 educational psychologist to 8,000 children. A few LEA's, however, still operate at a ratio of 1 to 12,000 or worse. Similar variation is seen in the case-loads of advisers and educational welfare officers.

The branch of the LEA to which disruptive pupils are most likely to be referred is the educational (or school) psychology service. Educational psychologists are trained teachers. They have generally taken a BA degree in psychology, and a Masters degree in the application of psychology to education and child development. They have no statutory responsibilities, but the DES (1975) has made clear that they should advise the chief education officer whenever special education is being considered. Recent years have seen a strong movement within the profession away from a clinic-based treatment service towards a school and community-based advisory service (Gillham 1978). This stems from recognition that recommendations based on individual assessment have little value unless fully accepted by the teacher who will need to implement them. Rather than see a small number of pupils individually, time is better spent helping teachers themselves to assess the needs of disturbing pupils and to plan suitable programmes for them.

Educational welfare is another service which is becoming increasingly accessible to teachers. Long regarded as the Cinderella of the Social Services, its responsibilities have traditionally been confined to school attendance. In many areas, however, EWOs have started to undertake a wider range of activities, as advocated by the Local Government Training Board (1972) and by Fitzherbert (1977a, b). Galloway et al. (1981b, c) have argued that they can most usefully operate in partnership with teachers, to establish better cooperation and understanding between teachers and parents.

Local education authority advisers are sometimes another source of advice about disruptive pupils. They are seldom able to help with individual pupils, but may be in a position to contribute to in-service training programmes for year tutors or remedial teachers. They have usually had extensive teaching experience before becoming advisers, and may be able to offer a valuable analysis of ways in which school organisation and policy contribute to the problems under discussion.

Sources of help outside the local education authority
In many LEAs educational psychologists divide their time between the LEA's school-orientated psychological service and a child guidance clinic. The clinic team traditionally consists of a child psychiatrist, educational psychologist and social worker.

Although this pattern still receives considerable support (e.g. Cline 1980), it has been replaced in some areas by a system in which the LEA's educational psychology service and the area health authority's hospital departments of child psychiatry operate independently. Child guidance clinics and hospital child psychiatric out-patient clinics offer a diagnostic, and sometimes a treatment service. However, as we shall see shortly, the most widely offered forms of treatment are singularly unsuccessful with the majority of disruptive pupils referred by teachers. Nevertheless, the clinic team is able to investigate the possibility of medical problems aggravating, or even causing the child's disruptive behaviour. It can also offer parents social work or psychiatric support in their own right.

The area health authority's school health service is more accessible to teachers than child guidance or child psychiatric clinics. Whitmore (1974) argued that all disruptive pupils should be seen by a school doctor as well as by an educational psychologist. It is not clear that this is either desirable or practical as a general rule. Nevertheless informal discussion with the school doctor is often desirable, particularly when the doctor operates as a member of a team providing a comprehensive educational psychologist and social worker.

Some results of treatment
Until the early 1970s various forms of psychotherapy were the most widely practised forms of treatment in child guidance and child psychiatric clinics. This probably remains true today, though other approaches are gradually becoming more popular. An influential study by Levitt (1957) reviewed articles which described the results of psychotherapy with children between 1929 and 1955. In all, almost 8,000 children had received treatment. Of these, two-thirds were rated improved by the end of treatment, and three-quarters at follow-up. The critical point, though, was that similar improvement rates

were found in children who were offered treatment but withdrew before it began. Subsequently Levitt (1963) attempted a more sophisticated analysis, relating progress in psychotherapy to the child's original symptoms. His review of twenty-two studies concluded that children with readily identified symptoms such as enuresis or school phobia had a good prognosis. In contrast, children with socially more disruptive problems, such as delinquency, were significantly less likely to improve during or after psychotherapy. These, of course, are the children who are most likely to be considered disruptive at school.

Levitt's conclusions about the sort of child who might benefit from psychotherapy have been criticised (Hood-Williams 1960; Wright et al. 1976). His results were, however, strongly supported by Robins (1966, 1972) in a long-term follow-up of children treated in a child guidance clinic in St Louis, USA. Children seen for neurotic disturbances had almost as good adult adjustment as the comparison group of 'normal' children matched for IQ, race, age and neighbourhood. Children seen for anti-social behaviour, on the other hand, were more likely to have received in-patient psychiatric treatment as adults, to have been in trouble with the police, to have a poor employment record and to experience difficulty in family relationships as adults. Similar results have been reported in England (Shepherd et al. 1971; Mitchell and Rosa 1981).

To summarise, the outlook for children referred for psychotherapy or treatment in child guidance clinics is not altogether bleak (Eisenberg et al. 1965). Children with emotional or 'neurotic' types of problem stand a good chance of improving more rapidly with individual or family psychotherapy than without treatment. However, children whose behaviour most disturbs their teachers are apparently unlikely to benefit from the sort of individual and family therapy offered by most child guidance clinics and child psychiatric services.

Special schools and units

Special schools
Removing a severely disruptive pupil to a special school may reduce pressure on the original school. Whether this also helps the pupil is less clear. Most studies agree that two-thirds of boys leaving approved schools (or, since the 1969 Children's and Young Persons' Act, community homes with education on the premises,) are in further trouble with the police within two years (HMSO 1972). This figure is remarkably stable, irrespective of the school's regime. Thus, neither a so-called 'therapeutic community' (Cornish and Clarke 1975;

McMichael 1974), nor family grouping in a junior approved school (Craft 1965), achieved better than average results in terms of subsequent conviction rates. Clarke and Cornish (1978) argue that the ineffectiveness of *any* residential treatment is predictable, since it fails to take account of the stimuli which elicit delinquent behaviour. We shall return to this point.

Systematic research on the achievements of special schools for maladjusted children is conspicuously lacking. A study in London found that children referred to day special schools tended to be too timid or withdrawn to cope with ordinary school life, while children referred to residential schools were more likely to be regarded as delinquent or beyond control (ILEA 1965). If Levitt (1963) and Robins (1966) are correct, the day school pupils should have a better prognosis. Yet only 16 per cent of leavers returned to ordinary schools. Cooling (1974) reported 21 per cent of leavers from residential special schools returning to ordinary schools. The limited available evidence is reviewed by Galloway and Goodwin (1979). Although some schools have reported encouraging results (e.g. Burland 1978), the overall picture is not encouraging.

Off-site units

In the late 1960s and 1970s it became clear that existing special school facilities could not cope with the older and more overtly threatening pupils about whom schools were starting to complain. Nor could these pupils any longer be transferred to, or left in the 'non-academic' streams of secondary moderns. Either the special school system must expand, or separate facilities must be created for this new category of 'special' pupil.

Education officers gradually realised that it was usually cheaper and always administratively easier to open special centres for disruptive adolescents rather than expand the special school system. The reasons lie in the small print of the 1944 Education Act, and need not concern us here. The distinction was largely administrative. Units were faced with fewer staffing constraints in the form of recommendations on pupil : teacher ratios in special schools (DES 1973). They could be more flexible in their admission and discharge procedures. Pupils would always remain on the roll of their original school, to which it was theoretically hoped they would return. Having established these un'ts LEAs found themselves forced to deny that they catered for maladjusted children, since maladjusted children must – under the 1944 Act – be educated in special schools or classes for the maladjusted.

Her Majesty's Inspectorate (HMI) responded to public and professional interest in this increasingly popular form of provision, by carrying out an inquiry into existing 'behavioural units'. They showed that 72 per cent of 96 LEAs surveyed had established units by 1976. Just over three-quarters of the 239 units served more than one school.

Her Majesty's Inspectorate were critical of the quality of buildings provided for units, and to a lesser extent of inadequate accommodation for particular subjects. Some of the units appeared to receive insufficient funds, both for capital and for day-to-day expenditure. There was some evidence that pupils attended the units more regularly than they had attended their previous schools, but no comparative figures were available. With masterly diplomacy, HMI described the number of pupils returning to their previous ordinary schools as 'difficult to calculate'. They did note, however, that units catering for secondary pupils contained a high proportion of disaffected fourteen-to sixteen-year-olds, for whom return was unlikely. A wide range of academic subjects was offered across the units which HMI visited, but the number provided in individual units was inevitably small.

Descriptive accounts of off-site units are not hard to find (e.g. Galway 1979; White and Brockington 1978; Rowan 1976; Dain 1977; Pick 1974; Taylor et al. 1979). Yet systematic evaluation appears to be almost non-existent. Grunsell (1978) gives a vivid account of the Islington Centre in London, catering mainly for truants with an additional history of disruptive behaviour. The Centre's relatively unstructured approach tolerated a wide range of behaviour. Grunsell's descriptions of the pupils are reminiscent of those of the pioneer workers with maladjusted children (e.g. Wills 1941; Lane 1928).

A consistent but disappointing trend from the limited available literature is that successful return to school is seldom achieved. Two exceptions to this general tendency are the Key Centre in Birmingham and the Hungerford Centre in London (Dain 1977; Lane 1977; Lane and Millar 1977; Rowan 1976). Both centres are also unusual in offering short-term treatment, and in accepting pupils only if the referring schools agree to their early return.

On-site groups
The opening of special schools for maladjusted pupils and centres for disruptive pupils was widely welcomed by teachers in ordinary schools. Their enthusiasm wavered, however, when they realised that they could realistically expect only one or two children a year to be transferred to these schools or centres from their own schools. Thus, while LEAs were opening special units, head-teachers were opening special groups. These groups were usually intended to supplement the

school's disciplinary and/or pastoral care networks. They catered for the school's own pupils.

The first LEA to explore the possibility of special groups for disruptive or maladjusted children in primary schools was West Sussex (Labon 1973). Teachers were appointed by the head, as much for their personal maturity as for their teaching ability. The aims were explicitly therapeutic; the severity of a child's problems was less important than whether he would benefit from admission. There was an emphasis on creative activities which would help the children to relax, talk about themselves and establish cooperative relationships with the teacher and with each other. Each group maintained regular contact with educational psychologists, who provided in-service seminars for the teachers.

A similar philosophy lay behind one of the early secondary school groups, at Brislington school in Bristol (Jones 1971; 1973; 1974). Whereas all pupils in the West Sussex groups attended part-time, at Brislington they attended full-time, for an average of nine months. Emphasis was placed on a phased return to ordinary lessons. Even when a pupil was attending ordinary lessons full-time, the group would still be available for support if needed; there would never be final discharge. Both in West Sussex and at Brislington, cooperation of class or subject teachers was regarded as essential. Moreover, it was hoped that the groups would influence their attitudes and practices. Nevertheless, the class teacher's role appeared peripheral to that of the group teacher, in the sense that the latter had primary responsibility for helping the child adjust to the demands and expectations of the school's mainstream.

Labon's (1974) study of the West Sussex groups showed that headteachers thought up to two-thirds of pupils improved in their relationships with other children and with adults. The children least likely to benefit were those who had displayed 'acting out behaviour disorders' prior to admission. This was confirmed by Archer (1973) who showed that introverts were more likely to benefit from attending an adjustment group than extroverts. A study by Vacc (1968) in America found that children improved while attending a special group, but did not maintain this improvement on return to an ordinary class (Vacc 1972).

As many on-site groups have been established on a head-teacher's own initiative, they were not necessarily included in the study by HMI (1978). Although reliable figures are lacking, there is no doubt that they have increased dramatically. The Pack Report on truancy and indiscipline in Scotland (Scottish Education Department 1977) encouraged this trend, as have speakers at teachers' conferences (e.g.

Lodge 1977). It would be naïve to expect that special groups have become popular as a result of the success of early ventures such as those in West Sussex and Brislington. The wider educational and social pressures which were discussed in the Introduction are at least as important.

As with off-site units, descriptive accounts of special groups are not hard to find (e.g. Holman and Libretto 1979), but systematic evaluation is conspicuously lacking. There is widespread concern that special groups may function as 'sin-bins' whose function is simply to contain trouble-makers. Nevertheless, all the articles we have traced describe groups with wider, more constructive aims than punishment or containment. There are two possible reasons. One is that all existing groups do in fact have broader educational and therapeutic aims. The second is that no teacher who confines himself to a custodial role will be keen to publicise what he is doing.

The school's contribution; sociological and educational perspectives

Introduction
The assessment and treatment services we have described so far focus on managing, or treating disruptive behaviour after it has occurred. This is a little like driving an ambulance to the casualty at the bottom of the cliff. The trouble is that preventing disruptive behaviour from occurring in the first place is a little like the abolition of war, poverty and injustice – a lovely idea, but until someone tells us how to do it we must continue to drive the ambulance.

It would be altogether too optimistic to say that recent educational and sociological research has shown how disruptive behaviour can be prevented. Nevertheless we are starting to understand how schools may in fact facilitate the disruptive behaviour which they seek to prevent. In addition, an important series of research projects has focused on the organisation, policies and practices of 'successful' schools.

Labelling theory and the development of deviance
Some writers see conflict between teachers and pupils as an inevitable result of the educational process. Thus Newman and Wilkins (1974) argue that one, often unstated, aim of education is to close the generation gap. 'Yet the inevitable politics of the situation,' they claim, 'dictate that children be educated as one educates servants; in the sense that children are kept in submission, they are fed (unavoidably) only

particular kinds of reality.' School, Newman and Wilkins argue, has something in common with the 'total institution' described by Goffman (1961). Goffman's definition of a 'total institution' is 'a place of residence and work where a large number of like-situated individuals, cut off from the wider society for an appreciable period of time, together lead an enclosed, formally-administered round of life'. Such a system requires rules; the paradox is that obedience to rules logically implies the possibility of disobedience. Punishment implies the possibility of reform; it also involves the possibility of rebellion by pupils who question teachers' right to punish.

Under this model, the more 'closed' the school in its administration and relationships with 'outsiders' such as parents and community figures, the stronger the probability that some pupils will behave in a deviant way. In other words, the school's own rules and expectations create deviance. A pupil who insists that he is an atheist will go unnoticed at one school. In a Roman Catholic school, on the other hand, his atheism constitutes a fundamental challenge, not only to Higher authority, but also to the school's authority.

The link between punishment and rebellion by pupils who question the teachers' right to punish had previously been inferred by Werthman (1963). He maintained that school discipline depends on pupils accepting the legitimacy of the teacher's authority. Some pupils refuse to accept that teachers are entitled to exert authority simply by virtue of being teachers. These are the pupils who teachers are likely to regard as deviant.

Cicourel and Kitsuse (1968) took this argument a stage further in their analysis of secondary school organisation and its power to encourage the emergence of the deviant behaviour which its stated aim is to discourage. Labelling a pupil, for example, as 'a slow learner', 'truant', 'in need of counselling', 'from a bad home' can actively assist in launching him on a school career of delinquency and failure. When contacts between the school and outside agencies are close and informal, the dangers are enhanced. In other words, once the individual has been labelled, he may be expected to live up, or down, to his label.

The term 'secondary deviance' has been used to describe this process. Lemert (1967) argued that initial deviance elicits a response from authority or from society. This response can then elicit further deviant actions, for example when the pupil rebels against punishment or conforms to his new role as a trouble-maker. Thus, labelling and deviance can form a vicious circle, especially when the pupil incorporates the label into his own perception of himself (Rotenberg 1974).

Case studies of individual schools

The process just described has been described in a participant–observer study of an English secondary school. Hargreaves (1967) was able to carry out extensive interviews with pupils and teachers in the course of a year's observation of the school's life and work. He was able to demonstrate the existence of an anti-school subculture among older pupils in the lower-stream classes. Although the teachers argued that streaming was necessary because of the subculture, Hargreaves pointed out that the low-stream boys in their first two years were not generally hostile towards the school. This hostility developed from recognition that they were no longer considered worth entering for public examinations. Having been 'written off' by the school, they responded by 'writing off' the school. Whether some forms of school organisation, such as streaming, do in fact facilitate the development in pupils of goals which are inconsistent with the school's stated goals is controversial. It seems possible that the subculture noted by Hargreaves developed because the pupils concerned felt that the school no longer valued them, providing them with no opportunity to achieve success. If so, this is a statement about the teachers' value system, not about the policy of streaming as such, though the two are in practice likely to be linked. More recently Hargreaves and his colleagues (1975) have described in more detail the development of deviance as perceived by teachers. In particular they explain how the teacher's initial reaction to deviant behaviour can create further problems ('secondary deviance') by uniting the pupils in their opposition to the school's value system.

Teachers' reports about disruptive behaviour in their classes were investigated systematically by Lawrence et al. (1978). Their work is of interest for identifying some of the ways in which a school's organisation can create the problems which it subsequently spends a lot of time trying to solve. A noticeable example was the tendency for relatively minor incidents to escalate from a matter between the pupil and his teacher, which could possibly have been dealt with at this personal level, to a confrontation between the pupil and the school's authority system (Lawrence et al. 1977). Thus, pupils could be sent to the hall following unacceptable behaviour in class. In the hall, their names would be written in an 'exclusion book' by a deputy head, who might then decide to impose her own sanction. On some occasions the problem escalated rapidly, with the pupil failing to turn up for detention, then refusing to accept corporal punishment, so that exclusion became the only remaining alternative left to the school. Yet by the time this stage was reached, the incident which precipitated the train of events leading to the decision to cane was almost forgotten. Our own observations from interviews with suspended pupils are, of course, consistent with this (see Ch. 3).

Comparisons between schools

Teachers seldom have difficulty in accepting the school's influence over pupils' behaviour at school. They are understandably much more sceptical about its influence over their behaviour out of school. Yet the evidence that schools influence their pupil's behaviour outside the school itself is now strong. The first substantial evidence about the school's influence on delinquency rates came from the London Borough of Tower Hamlets (Power et al. 1967, 1972; Phillipson 1971). These reports noted major differences between secondary schools in an inner-city area in the number of pupils appearing before juvenile courts, which could not be attributed to differences in the pupils or their backgrounds.

Power's conclusions were attacked on methodological grounds by Baldwin (1972), and other studies in London have suggested that high-delinquency schools tend to admit more pupils who might be considered 'at risk' of delinquency on the basis of their home district (Farrington 1972; West and Farrington 1973). Rutter et al. (1979), however, have noted that examination of West and Farrington's data reveals greater differences between schools than they acknowledge. Moreover, Power's original conclusions were strongly supported by Gath et al. (1972, 1977). They noted a closer association between high delinquency rates in a school and high rates of referral to child psychiatric clinics, neither of which could be explained by differences between the schools' catchment areas. In addition, a series of studies in a South Wales mining valley has shown consistent variation in delinquency rates and school attendance rates between secondary modern schools serving a fairly homogeneous population (Reynolds 1976; Reynolds et al. 1976; Reynolds and Murgatroyd 1977).

Studies of children's behaviour at both primary and secondary schools have confirmed the implication from these studies that schools exert an important influence over their pupils' social adjustment. More important, studies based on observation or direct information from pupils can start to identify the characteristics of schools which do not experience severe problems from disruptive behaviour – and vice versa. Heal (1978) compared the reports of pupils at thirteen primary schools on their own deviant behaviour. The level of misbehaviour varied significantly from school to school, and could not be explained by the pupils' backgrounds. Evidence from the schools enabled him to conclude that high rates of misbehaviour were associated with more formal punishment systems and with the temporary accommodation brought in to cope with a large increase in pupil numbers in some schools.

Finlayson and Loughran (1976) used a school climate index (Finlayson 1973) to compare the ways in which pupils attending two high-delinquency and two low-delinquency schools perceived their school. An important finding was that the poor relationships associated with high delinquency levels were between teachers and their classes, *not* between teachers and individual pupils. Teachers at the high-delinquency schools were not seen as less caring towards individuals; in at least one school the reverse seemed to apply. In contrast, they *were* seen as defensive and authoritarian in their interaction with their classes. The authors comment: 'in such a cycle the repressive measures which the teachers are perceived to adopt could themselves be an important factor in the contribution which the high delinquency schools seem to make to inflating their delinquency problems.' One implication here is that establishing an elaborate guidance and counselling system in a school will be unlikely to reduce disruptive, delinquent behaviour if the primary objective is to provide a personal service to children in need. Providing such a service may be desirable for other reasons, but it should not, from this evidence, expect to tackle the issues which precipitate disruptive behaviour in the first place.

This conclusion is supported by results from a study of truancy (Reynolds and Murgatroyd 1977). Schools with a marked truancy problem tended to deal with it at the 'middle management' level of year tutor or head of house. In contrast, two-thirds of schools which did not have a self-defined truancy problem, made class teachers responsible for dealing with truants. Of course, the truancy problem might have led some schools to allocate this responsibility to middle management, yet the authors found that the class teachers' responsibilities had actually declined in some schools, raising the possibility that the growth in middle management had actually caused the increased truancy rates.

Finlayson's and Loughran's study was important for directing attention towards relationships in the classroom. It was not, however, able to identify the reasons why defensive, authoritarian relationships developed between pupils and teachers. While not investigating this question specifically, other research has started to fill in some of the gaps.

A consistent, but superficially surprising, finding is that structural variables, such as age and quality of buildings are relatively unimportant as determinants of pupils' behaviour, or of their educational attainments. It was this that led Coleman (1966 et al) and Plowden

(DES 1967) to dismiss differences between schools as relatively trivial in their effect on children. It is now clear that these reports failed to investigate the critical variables. Encouragingly, teachers have much more control over the critical variables than over the structural state of the school buildings.

Reynolds and Murgatroyd (1977) found a mild trend for smaller schools to have higher attendance rates. A statistical analysis, however, demonstrated that it was the rules operated by the school which were of most importance. Specifically, the successful schools tended to have prefect systems, thus involving pupils in the running of the school, to enforce uniform for younger pupils and to have low corporal punishment rates. In an earlier report on the same group of studies, Reynolds (1976) suggested that schools with serious discipline problems were characterised by inflexible relationships between pupils and teachers. If, for example, the teachers insisted on fifteen- or sixteen-year-olds observing the minutiae of school uniform as strictly as eleven-year-olds, the older pupils would in turn become less amenable in other teacher-directed activities. Teacher–pupil relationships in the successful schools in Reynolds' study were characterised by a 'truce' in which each side tacitly agreed not to make demands which the other would regard as unreasonable.

The most influential study of school influences on pupils' performance was carried out by Rutter et al. (1979) in a comparative study of ten schools in South London. The study originated in Rutter's earlier epidemiological work, described in Chapter 1. He followed up the progress of the ten-year-olds in his original sample when they had reached the age of fourteen. Statistical analysis showed that the behaviour reported by teachers for the ten-year-olds could be used to predict the number of pupils who would be behaving in a deviant way at fourteen. The results revealed startling variation between schools (Rutter 1977). Some schools reported a much higher incidence of deviance than was predicted, others a much lower incidence.

In their subsequent intensive study of twelve schools Rutter et al. (1979) illustrated marked differences between schools in the pupils' attainments and behaviour, and showed that these could not all be attributed to differences in pupils' intake. They then studied the formal and informal organisation of each school, thus building up a profile of policies and practices associated with high and low standards. The results are of immense importance, yet a summary may sound almost banal in its predictability. In the most successful schools there was a prompt start to lessons, a strong emphasis on academic progress and attainments, generally low frequency of punishment but high rate of recognition for positive achievements, well-cared-for buildings and a feeling by pupils that they could approach teachers with a personal problem. As in other studies, structural variables such as school size and age of buildings, and organisational variables, such as whether welfare was organised on a house or year system, seemed relatively unimportant.

In other words, the twelve schools did not differ significantly in the formal aspects of schooling, such as the buildings, the curriculum, even the rules. What mattered far more was a wide range of teaching practices which together created each school's ethos or 'hidden curriculum'. This was reflected in some interesting ways. More work by pupils was visible on walls in successful schools. Pot plants were also in evidence – perhaps because the prevailing ethos at the unsuccessful schools would have ensured their destruction!

Most of the research described so far was carried out in secondary schools. Bennett (1976) studied the association between teachers' styles and pupils' performance in thirty-seven primary schools. Twelve categories of teaching style were derived from a questionnaire survey on issues such as the curriculum, teaching method, discipline, allocation of teaching time and opinion on educational topics. The results of tests in English, reading and maths showed that children in formal classes tended to make more progress in English and maths than children in classes with a mixture of formal and informal approaches, or in informal classes. The mixed classes seemed to favour progress in reading. A study of teacher–pupil interaction in a smaller sample of classes suggested that teaching style exerted a greater influence over pupils' behaviour than personality differences in the children.

Bennett's study has been sharply criticised on methodological grounds (Rogers and Barron 1976). He has since re-examined his data and admitted to errors in his earlier analysis. His work nevertheless illustrates the teacher's influence on pupils' attainments and behaviour, from a different perspective to that adopted by the other studies we have mentioned.

Implications

Overview

Power et al. (1967) aroused the wrath of the teachers' unions with their suggestion that some schools might encourage delinquency in their pupils. Had they entitled their article: 'Delinquency prevention by schools in Tower Hamlets', they might not have been banned from carrying out further research. Yet they could have reported precisely the same results! They would simply have needed to draw attention to schools with exceptionally low delinquency rates, rather than schools with exceptionally high rates. The implication is that we should emphasise the information obtained about successful schools. Teachers cannot raise their standards unless they know what they are aiming at.

Discipline and pastoral care

A side-effect of secondary school reorganisation into a comprehensive system was an expansion in the number of posts with special responsibility for pastoral care. It would be cynical and untrue to say that pastoral care was invented to cater for the problems caused by large comprehensive schools. It would be cynical but true to say that no one talked much about pastoral care until the formation of comprehensive schools, and that these schools saw pastoral care develop into a specialist field in its own right.

In some schools this development has created as many problems as it has solved. We will only mention three here. First, the alternative career ladder has created divisions between 'pastoral' and 'subject' specialists. Second, it has led to an entirely spurious distinction between discipline and pastoral care. Third, the existence of posts with special responsibility for pastoral care has implicitly reduced the importance of the basic unit of pastoral care, namely the class tutor and subject teacher. The attitude: 'they get paid for it; let them do it', is understandable, but has unfortunate effects.

Galloway (1980b) describes the pressures on a year tutor or head of house who sees her responsibility as dealing personally with the problems of pupils in her year. All too easily she can find herself swamped with complaints from colleagues about 'her' pupils. Overwhelmed by the stresses she discovers in their backgrounds, she can rapidly find herself working as a cross between an unqualified counsellor (with pupils) and a volunteer in the Citizens' Advice Bureau (with parents). She will be in danger of working herself to an early coronary, losing much of her credibility as a teacher in the process.

The implication is not that year tutors as such are ineffective, and certainly not that they are unnecessary. It is rather that they should see their primary responsibility as coordinating the work of a team of form tutors and subject teachers. The form tutor needs to know her pupils as individuals. She needs to know the child who is temperamentally anxious, who will take short cuts if given half a chance, who adopts the role of class clown to hide his fear of failure, who cannot be expected to give his best because of troubles at home. Or to put all this more pretentiously, she needs to take pastoral care seriously. Described in this way, we can see why good discipline is wasted educationally unless combined with good pastoral care. Equally, good pastoral care is probably impossible and certainly ineffective without good discipline.

Just as discipline and pastoral care cannot sensibly be divorced, so pastoral care and educational progress are indissolubly linked. Headteachers of two Sheffield secondary schools told us of the consternation that had greeted their instruction that form tutors should ensure that pupils were completing homework. Many teachers resented this as an intrusion into their own field of expertise and responsibility. What was the point in a junior teacher in the modern languages department checking up that her form tutor group was completing homework set by the head of the maths department? The point was very simple. Failure to complete homework indicated the possibility of poor cooperation between home and school, or of poor attitudes towards school. These would need investigating, to see whether the problem was confined to maths, or extended into other curriculum areas, affecting the student's overall progress and adjustment.

Attempts to relate school discipline policies to pupils' behaviour and attainments run into immediate difficulty over the definition of discipline. Most studies side-step the problem by investigating the association between *punishment* policies and pupils' behaviour. Clegg and Megson (1968) found a positive correlation between the incidence of juvenile delinquency in a school's pupils and the school's use of corporal punishment. The most successful schools on several measures in David Reynolds' study of nine secondary moderns in South Wales had low rates of corporal punishment. In contrast, Rutter et al. (1979) found no evidence that any particular method of punishment affected the pupils' behaviour and attainment. Setting high academic standards, high rates of recognition for good work, and a feeling by pupils that they could approach a teacher with a personal problem appeared more important than the method of punishment. They also found no relationship between their measures of pupils' performance and the formal organisation of pastoral care.

Since it appears relatively unsupported by research, how can we justify our argument that pastoral care should be centred on the form tutor, with the year tutor or head of house taking a coordinating role? The answer is that research *does* support our view that the key to successful discipline and pastoral care is at the chalk face, however it may be organised from an administrative viewpoint. In Rutter's most successful schools, teachers set high standards, praised pupils for achieving them and created a climate in which pupils felt they could bring a personal problem to a teacher. Reynolds' (1976) most successful schools set clear rules, but were flexible in enforcing them, recognising how their pupils' values changed as they grew older. Finlayson and Loughran (1976) found that caring attitudes on an individual basis did not compensate for poor relationships between teachers and their classes.

If the key to discipline and pastoral care is at classroom level, it seems logical to recognise this in the formal organisation of the school's pastoral care support system. Yet we also need to consider the nature of teacher–pupil interaction in the classroom in order to arrive at a clearer understanding of disruptive behaviour and its management on a day-to-day basis. Paradoxically, this can illustrate how teachers unintentionally facilitate the behaviour they want to discourage, at the same time as illustrating some of the practices which maintain stable behaviour. Clearly there may always be some pupils who need to be removed temporarily from their class – or whose teachers need them to be removed. Special groups may cater for these pupils, but they cannot compensate for weaknesses in the school's discipline and pastoral care procedures.

Conclusions

Is the failure of treatment inevitable?
The evidence suggests strongly that overtly disruptive pupils are unlikely to benefit from 'talk' treatments such as counselling or psychotherapy. The limited evidence on the progress of children attending special groups also suggests that withdrawn or 'neurotic' children are more likely to benefit than those with more explicit, outwardly directed behaviour problems. However, the picture is not altogether gloomy. Since the 1960s interest in social learning has led to extensive research on aggressive behaviour and on ways it can be contained.

Yule (1978) in a useful review identified seven critical issues in social learning theory approaches to the management of aggression. Briefly, they are:

1. aggression is not a personality trait, but behaviour which must be studied in the context in which it occurs;
2. a central characteristic of aggressive behaviour is that it is extreme; for example, most young children sometimes push or shove, but the child who pushes hard and frequently is likely to be labelled aggressive;
3. aggressive behaviour demands a response from other children or from adults, but this response frequently reinforces the undesirable behaviour;

4. consequently, we should investigate how most children do control aggressive tendencies, rather than why a minority does not;
5. changing the child's behaviour in one setting will not necessarily lead to a similar change in a different setting, since children learn to behave in different ways according to the circumstances;
6. in planning treatment, we need not only to identify and encourage pro-social aspects of the child's behaviour, but also to teach him how to inhibit anti-social behaviour;
7. punishment is sometimes necessary as part of a wider treatment programme, but its effectiveness depends on 'timing, severity, consistency and identification of alternative behaviours'; (one might perhaps add that Yule is not endorsing corporal punishment here).

The starting-point for treatment derived from social learning theory is a careful 'behavioural analysis'. This, quite literally, aims to analyse the behaviour of all the people involved in the problem, and how they interact with each other. The behavioural analysis enables the teacher or psychologist to draw up a behaviour modification programme to tackle the problem in question. A project which has used these principles successfully with disruptive pupils referred to an off-site unit is the Hungerford Centre in London (Lane 1977; Lane and Millar 1977; Rowan 1976). Burland (1978) has described their use in Chelfham Mill School, a residential school for maladjusted boys of low or average intelligence. The most well-known behavioural programme for teaching delinquent pupils outside the school setting is Achievement Place in Kansas (Wolf et al. 1975; Phillips 1968; Phillips et al. 1973, 1976; Fixsen et al. 1973). This is a residential hostel catering for up to eight boys aged twelve to fifteen. An underlying aim in treatment is to teach the boys the skills necessary for successful performance in the wide range of situations in which they have previously failed.

Behavioural principles have been used quite extensively both in ordinary and in special school classrooms (e.g. O'Leary and O'Leary 1979; Kounin 1970; New Zealand Educational Institute 1975). It is worth noting that classroom behavioural analysis owes much to the analysis of classroom interaction in general (e.g. Flanders 1970; Delamont 1976). The relevance of this approach to discipline and pastoral care is not always made explicit. Behavioural analysis both requires and facilitates a clearer understanding of the individual pupil's needs and of his background. In planning treatment or management programmes for disruptive pupils, as in planning remedial procedures with poor readers, we need to know what motivates them. To make an informed guess at motivation we need information: (1) about the teacher's methods and objectives; (2) about social interaction in the school as a whole, and in the classroom in particular; (3) about the individual concerned, for example whether he is intellectually capable of understanding his class work; (4) about factors in his background which may affect his attitudes and adjustment at school.

Behavioural principles offer no panacea. Lane (1977) and Galloway (1977) mentioned a tendency to overemphasise behaviour modification techniques at the expense of the much more difficult behavioural analysis. Berger (1979) and Harrop (1980) have also described the dangers of over-enthusiastic use of behaviour modification techniques.

Closer specification of objectives

A consistent theme in social learning theory and in the behavioural principles derived from it is the need for a succinct, unambiguous specification of objectives. Her Majesty's Inspectorate (1978) also called for clearer specification of aims after their study of behavioural units. The same point holds good for special groups based in the school they serve.

Golby (1979) suggests two questions which should be central to the planning of any unit or special group: 'What do pupils learn in this particular special unit?' and 'does what they learn in this special unit relate to what they might learn in the mainstream?' He argues that any departure from a common curriculum must be justified, since a comprehensive school should aim to develop a common curriculum for all its pupils. Conversely, if something works well in a unit, teachers should examine the implications for the common curriculum.

More provocatively, Lloyd-Smith (1979) maintains that units reflect a reduced willingness by teachers to tolerate deviant behaviour. He notes that specialists now exist to cater for children with problems (presumably in the form of year tutors, educational psychologists and so on), and suggests that in consequence class teachers can now more easily pass the buck on to specialist staff. 'Thus', he argues, 'what the DES refer to as behavioural units are as much a product of ideological beliefs among teachers and educational policy makers as of any demonstrable change in patterns of behaviour among children of school age'.

Lloyd-Smith's emphasis on ideological belief is important, since it pervades the literature on off-site units and special groups within the school. Yet scarcely anywhere do the authors acknowledge their beliefs. We would argue that the treatment orientation of some of the groups described in this chapter reflect outdated beliefs about the nature of maladjustment, since they are based on an intrapersonal medical model which underestimates the socialising influence of the school itself. It is clear that disruptive pupils do have special needs, but equally clear that the school as a social and educational community exerts a substantial influence on its pupils' adjustment.

Golby (1979) suggests that units are legitimate to people who take an optimistic view of the education system, since they support a basically settled regime. Similarly, they are legitimate to a pessimist, as they protect the vulnerable from the worst aspects of the school system. This is too sweeping. A carefully thought out educational philosophy may lead one head-teacher to establish a special group, and another head to refuse to consider doing so.

We need to know far more about the reasons for establishing a special group for disruptive pupils or – equally important – for not establishing one. We also need to know far more about the pastoral and disciplinary policies and practices of the schools with groups – and of schools which consider groups unnecessary and/or ineffective. Since groups admit pupils from the mainstream and, in most cases, hope to return them to the mainstream, we need more systematic information both on the nature of the problems presented by their pupils and on the way the groups tackle these problems.

The question is not whether or not groups are effective, but rather: (1) in what circumstances they can operate effectively; (2) in what circumstances they are likely to run into difficulties; (3) in what circumstances a group is simply unnecessary or inappropriate. The next three chapters describe an investigation which aimed to start answering some of these questions.

Chapter 5

Special groups in secondary schools in one local education authority

Introduction

Background

At the time of our inquiry, Sheffield LEA had roughly 105,000 children of school age. It was thus one of the larger authorities. Sheffield has never suffered from inner-city blight of the sort that has plagued Liverpool, Manchester or Birmingham, but contains its fair share of depressed, high-density housing estates with innumerable social problems. On local government reorganisation in 1974 Sheffield incorporated parts of the former West Riding. Some schools on the outer boundaries are set in almost rural surroundings. All secondary schools are mixed and comprehensive, though there are massive differences in social conditions between catchment areas. Independent schools provide no serious threat to the comprehensive nature of the system as a whole. There are no public schools within twenty miles, and only one girls' direct grant grammar school opted for independent status when offered the alternative of integration into the LEA.

The city has a long tradition of special education for maladjusted and ESN(M) pupils in separate special schools. In 1978 two day schools catered for maladjusted pupils, and one for pupils who were both maladjusted and ESN(M). In addition the LEA provided a school at an in-patient child psychiatric unit and at a medium-stay residential home for exceptionally difficult children who had been admitted to care. Educationally backward children, many of whom presented less severe behaviour problems, were catered for in four primary and three secondary day schools for ESN(M) pupils. Disruptive pupils whose disturbing behaviour was associated, however indirectly, with minor physical handicap or health problems could be placed in two schools for delicate pupils, one of which contained residential places.

It is therefore clear that Sheffield had generous special school provision for its disturbing pupils. It should also be made clear that the majority of places in all these schools, with the possible exceptions of those in the in-patient psychiatric unit and the social services children's home, were offered to pupils whose *schools* had requested their transfer. This is not to deny that many of these pupils lived in unsettled, stressful families. The point is simply that they were admitted because of the problems they presented at school, which were seen as a symptom of family or personality disturbance.

Yet exclusion and suspension still present an administrative headache to senior members of the LEA – with the clear implication that the pupils concerned have caused more than just administrative headaches in their original schools. The special schools were unable to cope with the majority of these pupils. The reason, mentioned in Chapter 3, was simply that they could rarely admit pupils of fourteen or over, who constituted the majority of pupils suspended from school.

One administrative response from the LEA was to set up an off-site centre for severely disruptive pupils. This served all secondary schools in the city. Another administrative response was to look sympathetically at requests by individual schools to establish their own special groups for difficult pupils. Initially this was prompted by the recommendations of an informal working party on problem pupils set up in 1973 under the chairmanship of a senior assistant education officer. As a result of inquiries in several schools, the working party received a number of proposals from head-teachers for experimental projects to cater for these children in the ordinary school setting. One project proposed by a primary school head was eventually set up in 1974 with funds provided by a national urban aid programme. Two more, based in secondary schools, were started in the same year with direct assistance from the LEA. One school had already established a group on the head's own initiative, without external assistance. In the next three years, four more schools started their own group. The groups went by a variety of names, ranging from 'the unit' to 'Mr X's group'. For the sake of simplicity they are all referred to here as special groups, or simply 'groups.'.

The interest of HMI in off-site behavioural units has already been noted. It was clear, however, that the same conclusions would not necessarily apply to the smaller groups which many schools were setting up informally. By the autumn of 1977, seven of Sheffield's thirty-nine secondary schools had established a special group. Other head-teachers were known to be considering the possibility of doing so. In contrast, a few heads were known to be strongly opposed to any measures which might explicitly identify, and hence legitimise, a group of disruptive children in their schools. A preliminary survey of existing groups was carried out in 1977 by David Galloway, then a psychologist in the LEA, and Brian Wilcox, the LEA's senior adviser for research and evaluation. This indicated the feasibility of a more detailed inquiry, which took place in 1978 and 1979 with assistance from the DES as part of a wider programme of research on disruptive behaviour and unauthorised absence from school (Galloway et al. 1978; Galloway 1981c).

Selection of schools

All seven secondary schools which had established special groups were selected for intensive study. In addition, three schools were selected whose head-teachers were known to oppose the idea of setting up a special group for disruptive pupils. Thus, there was no attempt at random selection. More than three head-teachers were known to have expressed reservations about special groups, though we had no way of knowing exactly how many opposed this form of provision. The three schools without groups were selected for additional reasons besides their head-teacher's opposition to the idea of setting up a group.

One school was selected partly because it had outstandingly good public examination results, partly because it suspended a relatively large number of pupils and partly because the head-teacher had abandoned the idea of a special group, having experimented with it several years earlier. Another school was known to have achieved a dramatic reduction in the number of persistent absentees between 1973 and 1976. The third school was completing a process of substantial reorganisation involving a merger between a former comprehensive and a former selective school. In addition, this was the only voluntary aided school selected, and was known to suspend an unusually small proportion of pupils.

Nature of the investigation

The way we selected schools had obvious implications for the nature of the subsequent research. Briefly, we were working on a case-history model, rather than attempting a systematic comparison between the schools. This is not to say that comparison is impossible. Indeed, to some extent it is inevitable. We were not, however, aiming at a statistical analysis which would show whether groups were, or were not, 'a good thing'. Instead we were aiming to describe the aims, objectives and methods, not only of the special groups themselves, but also of the pastoral and disciplinary network in their host schools. In this way we hoped to describe the circumstances in which they could achieve their stated objectives, and the obstacles they encountered on the way. Similarly, we were hoping to record some of the experiences of teachers and pupils in selected schools without groups, in order to describe the circumstances in which special groups were considered – and might actually be – unnecessary or inappropriate.

All ten schools we originally selected agreed to cooperate in the investigation. In addition to obtaining information from the LEA's records, we interviewed the head-teacher, a random sample of teachers throughout each school, and pupils in their first or second year at the school and in their final year. In the seven schools with special groups, a member of the research team spent a week observing the group in operation. She subsequently interviewed the pupils attending the group, and obtained further information about the pupils from the teacher in charge. The results are described in this chapter and in Chapters 6 and 7.

The schools and their catchment areas

Overview

What sort of school opened special groups for their disturbing pupils? What sort of catchment area did they serve? We started by looking at some fairly wide variables. It quickly became clear that the schools with groups varied in size, catchment area and policy. Thus, four were in the largest 33 per cent of the LEA's thirty-nine secondary schools, one was in the middle 34 per cent and two were in the smallest 33 per cent. Using the same divisions, four had an above-average number of pupils receiving free school meals on the basis of their parents' low income, two an average number, and one a below-average number. Similar variation was evident in the three schools without groups. One was in the largest 33 per cent in terms of pupils on roll, one in the middle 34 per cent and one in the smallest 33 per cent. Two had an average number of pupils receiving free school meals and one an above-average number.

Five of the seven schools with groups had split sites, though in all cases the principal buildings were within easy walking distance of each other. Only one of the schools without groups was on a split site. Four of the seven schools with special groups had above-average unauthorised absentee rates, and two below-average rates. Of the schools without groups, one had an above-average absentee rate while the other two were in the middle 34 per cent of the city's schools on this variable. Similar variations were seen in the schools' policy on uniform. In addition, head-teachers' statements on the LEA's curriculum notation guide (Wilcox and Eustace 1980) showed that schools with special groups and schools without them varied substantially in terms of policy on ability grouping, pastoral care and organisation of remedial teaching.

Head-teachers' perceptions of catchment areas

These preliminary observations indicated that schools which had established special groups were not responding to any common set of problems in their catchment areas, nor was their decision associated with any common set of policies within the school. The schools with groups differed in size, catchment area and formally stated policies – but so did the schools without groups. This was confirmed by the head-teachers' subjective assessment of problems in their catchment area.

The head of school H, which had no group, for example, mentioned two estates, both some distance from the school:

'Our problems don't come from any one area, but predominantly [from these] . . . not too many difficulties over attendance, but problems of behaviour and attitudes to school on the part of pupils and their families, accentuated by their attitude towards the area in which we are situated.'

Another head-teacher, this time of school B, whch did have a special group, also mentioned two specific districts in his catchment area:

'These children cause more problems than the rest of the school put together – disruptive, bullying, trouble with the police and so on.'

Problems arising from poverty, apathy and neglect were mentioned by heads of schools with and without special groups:

'low income, or they mishandle their income, or a combination of both . . . and a remarkably high percentage of broken homes, one-parent families and so on.' (The head of school I, with no special group.)

'Education has a low priority for many, and many have a limited understanding of what school is trying to do, based on their own limited experience many years ago before comprehensive education.' (Head of school C, with a special group.)

Head-teachers' aims in establishing special groups

Discipline for children and support for teachers

We asked head-teachers about their original reasons for establishing a special group, and about their underlying aims for the group at present. Two head-teachers could not comment on the initial reason for setting up a group as they had been appointed since it was established.

Three head-teachers were nevertheless clear that the group was set up explicitly as a sanction, a last 'last resort' before exclusion or suspension. In each case, the aims had since been modified or extended. Three head-teachers' comments are worth quoting, because they illustrate an important point about school-based groups for disruptive pupils.

School C: We started it, quite honestly, as a sanction – an alternative to exclusion and suspension – for those for whom all other forms of action had so far failed. It followed caning, detention, seeing parents and so on. But we gradually started picking up other children, and we are now seeing it as a teaching situation, staffed to cover more subjects in the curriculum.

School B: We started it as a half-way house for the disruptive pupil, between being fully in the system and being fully excluded. Since then we have widened its scope to embrace almost the full spectrum of problems in the school. It remains a half-way house when needed, but not exclusively any more. For instance [we admitted] a child who broke his leg and could not move around the school. With one girl, truancy was part of the problem, but it was more deep-seated; there were family problems and she wanted someone to talk to.

School A: Initial aims were two-fold: first to prevent the suspension of pupils, and concommitant with that to raise staff morale. I was under pressure from the staff to suspend, so the senior AEO and I had a chat about the issues, including the legal issues. I very much wanted to contain our own problems – it was better for the school, and the city and most of all the pupils. The third aim was to hopefully do something for the children – but I must admit that was bottom of the lot. We hoped to do something for the children, but the first aim was to raise morale of the staff and to protect the vast majority of the school from disruption without having to force our problems on anyone else. It's done that job now, and as a result the staff are much more capable of coping with normal disruption . . . the kind you will get anywhere from time to time; and as a result their tolerance level has been raised considerably – well more – astonishingly. Now the unit is becoming very much more directed to the withdrawn child; it's beginning to deal with non-attenders and kids who have voted with their feet – the kind of child who will stop away from school because he can't face it. We've got one or two down there now who had been away for a year, and I think that's great.

Some interesting points emerge from these three quotations. Each one implies that the group's initial aims were custodial – to prevent the need for exclusion or suspension. Each one implies that it subsequently became possible to extend the group's objectives to cater for a wider range of children with a more explicitly therapeutic orientation. None of these three schools initially saw the group as a long-term alternative to ordinary classes. Certainly the groups were custodial, but at the outset the head-teachers were clear that pupils would return to the mainstream after quite a short time. Initially there seemed to be greater faith in the value of short sharp shock than in the treatment of children with problems. The evolution of the objectives in these three groups suggests that having satisfactorily overcome the problems necessitating suspension, they were able to widen their horizons. Unfortunately the reality was more complicated.

We shall see in Chapter 6 that opening a special group did *not* lead to any reduction in the number of pupils suspended for disruptive behaviour. Yet it would be cynical and possibly untrue to say that these three groups broadened their horizons because they recognised they had failed in their initial aims. At least two of the three head-teachers seemed surprised by the evidence that opening the group had not been followed by a reduction in the number of pupils suspended.

The reason for the development from a relatively passive custodial role to a more extensive, and possibly therapeutic one, seemed rather to lie partly in the head-teacher's own educational philosophy, and partly in the personality and attitudes of the teacher in charge of each group. In each case the teacher in charge was appointed after many years of experience in the mainstream. The point is really rather obvious: few experienced teachers will be satisfied with an essentially passive custodial role. Moreover, a favourable teacher : pupils ratio ensures that the teachers quickly come to know their pupils as individuals. The philosophy of a 'short sharp shock' is very difficult to apply in such circumstances, not least because in a small group virtually all pupils are willing to cooperate without this sort of artificial and mutually unpleasant incentive.

From the head-teachers' point of view, extending the group's scope had obvious advantages, since a limited deterrent or custodial philosophy for the group was inconsistent with their philosophy on discipline and pastoral care for the school as a whole. This is a point to which we shall return in Chapter 6. First, though, we must look at the aims of the other four groups.

Treatment for children and support for teachers
The heads of four schools with groups defined their aims in terms of benefit to the pupils selected to attend, while not discounting the benefit to the wider school community. The head of school G said:

It was originally set up strictly for the disruptives . . . . I rule out what happens at some schools, leaving children to work outside the head's door. What I want is them to get some treatment, and I've said to the teacher in charge: 'your job is to work yourself out of a job' . . . . While it does have the backwash effect of enabling ordinary teaching to go on peacefully, that wasn't the purpose; it was for the benefit of the *children*.

The head of school G had set up a special group for disruptive pupils because he was dissatisfied with the policy of containment by senior staff. It was certainly not the case that he doubted the ability of his senior staff to contain their pupils, let alone his own ability, but rather that he felt that a large comprehensive school should offer something more constructive.

The group's social education role was developed by the head of school E:

The basic thing is to get the children to settle into the basic run of the school, and therefore of the general run of society, better than they seem to be doing at present. This may be because they are being a nuisance to teachers, but not necessarily so. Working with other people, children and adults, is a thing children have to learn to do at school. And if the group can help them to do it, it's good for the children and for the school.

One of the aims of a comprehensive school is to give its children the chance to develop to their utmost in any area in which they are capable of developing. So you are keeping an eye on the child as a whole person – and if he needs some additional social training, then this is what the group is for. We're not trying to make them all alike, but nevertheless you can't help giving some idea of what *you* think is right. We're trying to get them to have the capacity to choose whether or not they're going to fit into society – to give them the tools for reasonable living.

A more consciously therapeutic philosophy was put forward by the head of school D:

If children are taken into the group, there's something positive that can be done for them. The factors will vary. It may be a straight psychological problem, or school rejection . . . but not just for disruptive behaviour in the school.

This head-teacher made clear that many of the pupils admitted to the group *were* disruptive, but their behaviour was seen as the result of psychological or home background factors.

The head of school F went a stage further, describing the group's aims in terms of benefit to the withdrawn child who was *not* disruptive in the main body of the school:

The aim is to ease the transition back into school for those who have been withdrawn for various reasons, largely emotional or home background problems . . . [We wanted] to give the inadequate child the necessary one-to-one support contact with a member of staff; the aim is eventually to return the children to normal schooling, and to give them a retreat when this takes place.

The head of this school had no doubts that senior staff could deal adequately with any disciplinary problems that might arise. The school seldom needed to consider exclusion or suspension, although situated in an extremely disadvantaged area. On the other hand, it did have a major problem with unauthorised absence and many of the pupils experienced acutely stressful home circumstances which were reflected in their adjustment at school.

Conclusions

We have seen that the seven Sheffield secondary schools with special groups did not serve similar catchment areas, nor did they operate similar internal policies on discipline or pastoral care. The decision to establish a special group was idiosyncratic, in the sense that the precise motivation varied from school to school, and the majority of the city's schools had not taken steps to establish a group in the first place. At least four schools (schools A, B, C and G) set out with the explicit aim of containing troublesome pupils, but only school G was equally explicit from the outset about the group's aim to help the pupils concerned. The other head-teachers still acknowledged the implicit and complementary aims of deterring other pupils and supporting staff, but emphasised that they had either modified or extended these original aims. On the other hand, the original aims had not been entirely abandoned. The teacher in charge of school C's group described the group as 'semi-punitive', placing it half-way between school B, which in his view was wholly punitive, and school D which had a reputation in the city for its pupil-orientated, 'therapeutic' approach.

There was one issue on which all seven head-teachers were agreed. All seven groups were pupil-orientated, in the sense that the underlying aim was to help or persuade the pupil to adjust to the reality and demands of the school. The fact that they set about this task in different ways does not invalidate this argument. Before accepting as obvious the notion that recalcitrant or 'disturbed' pupils should be obliged to adjust to the reality and demands of the school, it is worth returning to Chapter 2.

We showed then that Sheffield secondary schools varied widely in the number of pupils suspended for disruptive behaviour, implying a possibility that a school's own policies and practices might exert a substantial influence on its pupils' behaviour. If this is valid, it follows that pupil-orientated groups are tackling the symptom rather than the cause of the symptom. An analogy with remedial teaching may clarify this point. At many schools children are withdrawn from ordinary lessons for remedial help. The hope is that they will eventually return to ordinary lessons after successful remediation. The research suggests that this can indeed happen, but that improvement will only be maintained if adequate follow-up is provided. An alternative model is to provide help in the lesson in which the pupil is failing. The remedial teacher's job is then to adapt the curriculum – or rather the way the curriculum is introduced – to the needs of the individual (Galloway and Goodwin 1979; Griffin 1979). If this analogy has any validity for special groups, we might predict that they would need to retain substantial contact with pupils after returning them to ordinary lessons. We might also expect to see their aims defined in terms of a 'cooling-off period' during which it would be possible to identify and deal with the principal stress points in the school as a whole. We shall return to this point in Chapter 6, but must first look at the day-to-day administration of the seven groups.

Administration of special groups

Accommodation
All seven groups were based on the campus of their host school, though in three cases in 'terrapins' separate from the main buildings. One group had originally been based in a separate building. This had contributed to poor communication and consequent tension between the special group and the host school. The difficulty was resolved when the special group moved into the main school buildings. The three special groups which remained in terrapins did not seem to have experienced similar problems.

The groups' classrooms varied in size. Two had extremely small rooms, less than half the size of an average classroom. One group teacher said he had deliberately asked for this particular room, in order to discourage the wide-spread 'dumping' of disruptive children. If everyone knew that only six children could be squeezed into the room, they could not pressurise him into taking more. He believed that a major part of his work lay in supporting teachers in the mainstream, and did not see how he could do this if he had a large unwieldy group to look after. The more usual practice was for the group to be based in an ordinary classroom, though one group also had the use of a smaller adjacent room.

Equipment and furnishing varied only slightly from group to group. All groups had desks or tables, but only two had comfortable chairs as well. One of these groups (in school F) had separated a quiet area from the main body of the classroom. In two groups the furnishings looked suspiciously as though they might have been cast-offs from other classes in the school. In general, though, the quality of furnishing in the group reflected that in the school as a whole. The general décor seemed to a greater extent to depend on the teacher in charge. The amount of pupils' work on the wall varied widely. In some groups it was almost non-existent, while at others it was displayed extensively. This is an issue to which we shall return later in the chapter when discussing the curriculum. At the risk of stating the obvious, none of the groups had facilities to cater for certain topics in a secondary school curriculum, such as science, domestic science and so on. None of the groups were originally intended as a long-term alternative to ordinary schooling, so it was argued that there was no need to provide separate facilities for subjects requiring specialist equipment. This, too, is an issue to which we return later in the chapter.

Financial backing

The LEA had assisted in staffing four of the groups. The mechanics of this were somewhat obscure. Information from head-teachers suggested that there had generally been some form of agreement whereby the school could appoint an additional teacher, or that the schools which theoretically were already overstaffed would not be put under pressure to reduce their establishment of teachers. One of these four schools also received a grant of £300 from the LEA to help with initial equipment and teaching materials. Three schools received no staffing assistance from the LEA. These schools did, however, receive grants ranging from £500 to £1,000 to help set up the group.

Apart from the question of staffing, to which we shall return again shortly, the group did not impose a major financial burden on these schools. Annual running costs from the school's capitation allowance ranged between £20–30 and £80–100. In most cases petty cash was available to the teacher in charge in the same way as to any other teacher in the school. Lack of money did not seem to present a major problem to the teachers in charge, though several seemed surprisingly uncertain how much they either needed or were entitled to. One head was happily puzzled by the group teacher's persistent failure to press him for additional money.

A criticism which HMI (1978) made of some off-site units was their inadequate financial support. On the surface, this problem did not seem to exist to the same extent in the Sheffield on-site groups. On the other hand, few of the seven Sheffield groups embarked on ambitious programmes of visits or other activities, away from the classroom base. Had they done so, their costs might have risen considerably. This too raises questions about the curriculum, to which we return later in this chapter.

Staffing

We have seen that the LEA made special provision to enable four schools to appoint a teacher for their group. The arrangement in two cases was that the LEA would sanction the appointment of one person on the basic salary for a qualified teacher, but that the school would complement this in order to appoint someone at a higher salary, in the light of their special responsibilities. The LEA allowed two schools to appoint teachers on Scale II, the smallest allowance for special responsibility, but one of these schools increased this allowance from its own resources to Scale IV. Althogether, three of the teachers in charge were paid a Scale II responsibility allowance, three were paid a Scale III allowance and one a Scale IV. This, however, takes no account of other staff employed in the group on a part-time basis. The overall picture is given in Table 5.1. On appointment one teacher had seven years of previous teaching experience; the others all had over ten years' previous experience. Only two teachers, however, had taken an additional qualification in a specialist area such as counselling or remedial teaching.

Table 5.1
Staffing of special groups in ordinary secondary schools

	School						
	A	B	C	D	E	F	G
Staffing assistance from LEA	Nil	I × Scale I teacher	Nil	I × Scale II teacher	I × Scale I teacher	I × Scale II teacher	Nil
Salary scale of teacher in charge	II	II	III	IV	III	II	III
Number of teachers in group (including teacher in charge)	2	5	8	2	8	2	1
Number of full-time equivalent teachers (including teachers in charge)	1.5	2	1.5	1.3	1.5	1.3	1

Having several teachers working part-time in the group was seen by head-teachers as a potential solution to a number of curriculum problems. It would also enable the teacher responsible for the group to spend some of his time teaching ordinary classes. In principle this could help to prevent his isolation from his colleagues, and give him a valuable break from pressures within the group. In fact, though, only three teachers in charge of a group regularly taught ordinary classes. A more critical issue for some head-teachers was that the teacher in charge should be given time for liaison with colleagues and/or with external agencies.

Running the groups

Admission policies

All groups had clear admission policies. Some were followed to the letter. Some followed the letter but not the spirit of the policy. The head of school B explained his policy:

> It's my decision and/or the deputy's. No one else is allowed to put people in there – it always goes through us. The reason originally was that I didn't want teachers shovelling children in. The general guide is that if we hadn't got a centre, would you recommend exclusion, but we don't always stick to that.

As we saw earlier, School B still used its special group as a half-way house between exclusion and ordinary lessons, but had started to admit a wider range of children, including school refusers and a boy with a broken leg. The admission procedures had the virtue of simplicity, but control rested very firmly with the head. Two schools set up a meeting to consider potential candidates. The head of school F explained:

> Admission is through a meeting of head-teacher, deputy heads and year tutor. These meetings are called when necessary... in emergency children are put in before a meeting, pending discussion at a meeting.

The formal policy on admission, however, tells us less than half the story. The policy itself was much less important than the manner of its implementation. The head of school B, for example, was determined not to allow staff to 'shovel' children into the group. This is doubtless an admirable sentiment, but heads and deputy heads are under pressure too. At two schools, though not at school B, it was clear that the group sometimes provided a convenient receptacle for troublesome children at a time of crisis. The crisis, moreover, might be caused less by the pupil's troublesome behaviour than by other unrelated pressures on a senior member of staff which prevented her from investigating and dealing with it at the time.

In principle, emergency admission of this sort is not undesirable. Yet when emergencies occur more than once or twice a year, one wonders whether an overhaul is needed. A satisfactory admission procedure depended on one of two conditions. Either admissions were channelled through one or two members of staff who would never allow themselves to be rushed into hasty decisions, or the group teacher himself needed to have sufficient confidence and status to resist emergency admission until the aims and objectives had been agreed.

The pupils
The seven special groups catered for substantially different numbers of children (Table 5.2). We obtained information from the teacher in charge about all pupils who spent at least a part of the autumn term 1978 in the group. We also calculated the teacher:pupil ratio in the week we spent observing each group in the same term. School G is omitted from these results, which are shown in Table 5.3. Its group had to close in the autumn term due to the illness of the teacher in charge, and only one pupil was in the 'group' in the week we spent observing in the spring term. Consequently, this pupil spent much of the week attached to the teacher responsible for the group while he took other classes. This clearly has a number of implications, which will be discussed in Chapter 6.

Table 5.2
Number of pupils attending each group in the autumn term 1978

	School						
	A	B	C	D	E	F	G*
Number of girls (top row) and boys (lower row) in group, full-time and/or part time for at least part of the term	1	6	0	1	1	14	2
	7	8	12	8	4	12	2
Number of pupils in group full-time for at least part of the term	7	11	12	6	4	17	3
Mean number of weeks in full-time attendance	6	3	13	19	5	3	3

* Spring term 1979.

Table 5.3
Average teacher : pupil ratio in the course of one week's observation in the autumn term 1978

	School					
	A	B	C	D	E	F
Teacher : pupil ratio	1 : 2.3	1 : 1.8	1 : 5.3	1 : 2.3	1 : 1.6	1 : 3.8

Except at school F, over three-quarters of the pupils spent a period in the group full-time before making a gradual return to ordinary lessons. Hence, the pupils listed in Table 5.2 as attending 'full-time and/ or part-time' include some who had been admitted earlier in the year, but were no longer attending full-time by the autumn term. The mean number of weeks spent in the group full-time refers to all pupils attending in the autumn term, irrespective of when they attended full-time. The ratio of boys to girls varied between groups, but could also vary from time to time within one group. This could reflect the current pressures in the school. Thus, school C was using its group to try to contain a group of older boys who had lost confidence that they could benefit from regular attendance or cooperative behaviour.

The pupils shown in Table 5.2 were not, of course, all attending the groups at the same time. This explains the astonishingly favourable teacher : pupil ratio in Table 5.3, which would be envied by teachers in special schools for maladjusted children. In these schools the recommended ratio is 1 : 7 (DES 1973). Our figures are perhaps artificially low, as they were based on the number of pupils actually attending rather than the number on the group's roll. It is also true that numbers fluctuated from month to month. Even after taking both these points into account, however, the staffing ratio remained extraordinarily favourable.

The groups catered for pupils of different ages. School E, for example, only accepted pupils in their first three years of secondary education. The head felt that staff could reason more successfully with older pupils. A further aim in concentrating on the younger age-group was to tackle children's problem behaviour before it became too firmly established, and thus prevent difficulties arising in the final two years. The groups in schools D and F catered for pupils of all ages, depending on the pupils' and the school's needs at the time. The remaining groups listed in Table 5.2 catered primarily, though not exclusively, for pupils in the last two years of compulsory education. The group in school G catered exclusively for older pupils.

Return to ordinary lessons: policy and practice

Table 5.2 shows that short-term full-time admission occurred in only three schools, B, F and G. As all schools were in theory committed to the principle of early return to ordinary lessons, this seems odd. The head of school D, where pupils spent an average of nineteen weeks in the group full-time certainly recognised this problem:

This is the big unexplored area – the next thing to look at. Attempts *are* made to reintegrate children, sometimes quite successfully but the policy needs looking at. We try to integrate them back *as soon as they are ready*, but a problem is that the teacher in charge hasn't the time to follow them in the normal curriculum and classroom situation.

Return to ordinary lessons was almost invariably arranged on a gradual basis. To understand why it was apparently achieved more quickly at some schools than at others, we need first to look again at the policy for the group in schools B, F and G. Next we shall look more closely at the procedures involved in arranging return to ordinary lessons, in order to identify the obstacles which made this hard to achieve in some schools.

At school B the head exerted strict control over entry, and with the help of a deputy head and the teacher in charge of the unit, monitored pupils' progress each week. He was quite determined that the special group would not be used as a long-term educational alternative to ordinary lessons.

There is a definite commitment: it is written up large: 'Thou shalt not be there as a terminal case!' It's sometimes a struggle. The majority want to get out as soon as they can, but we do get a few who resist going back [to ordinary lessons]. No one is allowed to think this is a nice convenient way of sorting their problems out.

School G also catered for seriously disruptive pupils in its group, but the question of return to ordinary lessons was to a much greater extent a matter for informal negotiation between the teacher in charge and his colleagues.

School F, in contrast, used the special group to offer occasional support to children under stress, usually arising from circumstances outside the school. With this aim, full-time attendance was often unnecessary or inappropriate. This group was also exceptional in two other ways. First, seven of the twenty-six pupils who spent at least part of the autumn term in the group had never attended full-time; they had always remained in ordinary lessons for at least part of each week. Second, twelve pupils had attended less than 20 out of a possible 120 attendances prior to being placed in the group. Just as school B acted as a half-way house between exclusion and ordinary lessons, so school F acted as one between full-time unauthorised absence and ordinary lessons. The success of both groups in this respect is discussed in the next chapter.

We did hear of pupils who attended the groups at school B and school F for prolonged periods, though not in the survey period, and only in exceptional circumstances. In the other four schools, however, it was much less unusual for pupils to spend a substantial period full-time in the group. One possible explanation could lie in the underlying aims of these groups. If the philosophy is essentially deterrent, then it could theoretically make sense to set a time-limit after which the pupil will return to the mainstream. While pupils are in the group, close supervision will not only encourage good behaviour and hard work, but also ensure that pupils want to earn their release. Something of this philosophy was evident in school B. Yet it was also evident in schools A and C, where pupils spent an average of six and thirteen weeks respectively as full-time pupils.

In contrast, if the underlying philosophy leads to the aim of treating the troubled child, then it seems logical that the child should remain in the group until he has responded to treatment. Something of this philosophy was evident in school D, where pupils spent an average of nineteen weeks in the group full-time. Yet it was also evident in school F, where they spent only 3.1 weeks. Thus, we cannot attribute the discrepancies to differing aims and objectives. Nor can we explain them in terms of the problems of the pupils admitted to the group. School B quite explicitly regarded its group as an alternative to suspension. Yet so did school C, where pupils spent an average of thirteen weeks as full-time members of the group. A look at the processes involved in return to ordinary lessons throws some light on the subject.

Again, school B's policy is instructive. The head told us:
First they generally go to selected lessons on 'Special Group report'. When they are out all the time they stay on Group report for a further week, then they report to the year tutor, which is less of an inconvenience for them.
There are two points to note here: (1) The pupils' progress in ordinary classes was closely followed by means of the 'Special Group report' system, whereby the child was required to give his teachers in ordinary classes a report form for completion at the end of each lesson. At the end of the day he had to take this form to the teacher in charge of the group. (2) After a week of satisfactory behaviour in the mainstream, his year tutor took over responsibility from the group teacher, but would continue to check up daily on his progress. This could

perhaps be viewed as commendably caring or unnecessarily coercive. It certainly shows careful planning.

A contrast was provided by the head of school C, who was having second thoughts about the principle of phased release from the group:

We are not using the idea of half-time attendance in the group now. To start with, it was a matter of earning reprieves, and they'd get a bit cocky. It wasn't sufficiently exacting; they just got the idea that if they kept their noses clean for a bit it would be all right ... I'm really not sure what we're going to do about this; I think not phased release – more a definite return.

The head of school C now saw the group as a rehabilitative project, not simply an alternative to exclusion. There were three problems. First, the implications appeared not to have been fully understood, let alone accepted, by all teachers. The teacher in charge described the problem succinctly:

When they go back into the rigours of normal school life, I know for a fact some teachers say: 'Oh my God, not him again!' It's a case of give a dog a bad name and it sticks.

The second problem was that the pupils themselves were insufficiently motivated to return to the mainstream. This is an issue to which we return in greater detail in Chapter 6. Finally, the longer a pupil remained out of the mainstream, the greater the curricular difficulties in arranging his return. We return to this point shortly.

Reasons for admission

The reasons for admitting pupils to the different groups have already been discussed in general terms, in relation to the group's aim and objectives. We are concerned here with the reasons in individual cases. We asked the teacher in charge of each group about the problems at school which had led to the decision to admit each pupil who attended for all or part of the autumn term. All group teachers gave more than one reason for most pupils. In Table 5.4 we show the most frequently stated reasons.

Although the numbers are extremely small, the table shows a discrepancy in school G between the number of pupils who were reported to have been disturbing normal teaching, and the number reported as having behaved aggressively or disruptively. The explanation is, of course, that the problems did not occur in lesson time, but in the lunch-hour or mid-morning or mid-afternoon breaks. The small proportion of pupils admitted to the group in school F for aggressive behaviour or for disturbing normal teaching indirectly confirms the emphasis in this group on providing support for children whose problems originated out of school. In addition, poor school attendance was

Table 5.4

Reasons for admission of pupils attending special groups in the autumn term 1978, as reported by teachers in charge

	Schools						
	A (N:8)	B (N:14)	C (N:12)	D (N:9)	E (N:5)	F (N:26)	G (N:4)
Poor school attendance (%)	50	43	33	44	40	73	50
Aggressive, disruptive behaviour (%)	75	64	75	66	40	8	50
Bad influence on peers (%)	63	79	66	33	40	8	0
Disturbing normal teaching (%)	75	71	66	66	40	8	25

frequently stated as the main reason for admission to this group, while in the other groups it was more often reported as a contributory reason.

Supervision in lunch-hour and breaks

If some pupils are admitted to a group because they have caused disturbances in the lunch-hour or break, it seems logical that they should be closely supervised at these times. Arranging this creates administrative problems for teachers, who need their own breaks, and can lead to union pressure if not carried out on a strictly voluntary basis. The only group which supervised all pupils' movements throughout the lunch-hour, and the mid-morning and mid-afternoon breaks was in school B. Such close supervision was, of course, consistent with the closely defined aim of this group. School E, whose group catered only for pupils up to the age of fourteen, insisted on most pupils in the group remaining under a teacher's direct supervision outside formal lesson times.

Interestingly, school A, many of whose pupils were apparently referred for disruptive behaviour in and out of class, insisted on all group pupils going home for lunch. The rationale was that they could not then be in trouble in or around the school. During the mid-morning and afternoon breaks, the pupils were supervised by one of the group's two teachers. Two groups appeared hardly ever to provide special supervision outside the classroom, and the remaining two teachers in charge reported that they occasionally provided supervision at these times but only when this was considered necessary for a special reason.

Contact with outside agencies

Teachers in charge varied radically in their contacts with external
agencies, either within the LEA or outside it. This reflected the head-
teacher's formal policy as much as the personal preference of the
teacher concerned. School B was at one extreme. No member of any
external agency was permitted to visit the group, and all inquiries
about pupils attending the group were directed to the head or deputy.
The group was established with staffing assistance from the senior
assistant education officer responsible for secondary schools, but it
was seen as a purely internal project requiring neither liaison with,
nor advice from, other branches of the LEA such as the advisers or
psychological services.

At the other extreme, the heads of schools D, E and F sought the
LEA's assistance in setting up the group after a great deal of discussion with – and in at least one case initiated by – the school's educational psychologist. The teachers in charge of these groups maintained
contact with their school's educational psychologist, either to discuss
the management of a particular child, or to consider more general
issues such as record-keeping, policy on admission and discharge and
so on. The teachers in these groups also attempted to liaise with social
workers, probation officers and members of other agencies who
already knew a pupil in the group.

These contacts with agencies outside the LEA were seldom com-
pletely satisfactory. The most frequent complaints were the high staff
turnover in some of the support services, difficulty in making contact
in the first place, and even greater difficulty in maintaining useful contact subsequently. The reasons are complex, and the problem is by no
means confined to special groups. It is, however, perhaps worth making the rather obvious point that children's lives outside school can
affect their performance in school and vice versa. Teachers and the
support services should have something to learn from each other. As
we have seen, there were no contacts with one group (school B). Two
other groups (schools A and C) had little contact. The teacher in
charge of school A's group preferred as a matter of principle not to see
specialist reports on pupils before their admission, since he felt this
could cloud his judgement. While sympathising with this view, one
also wonders whether advance information about a pupil's learning
and/or family problems might help in planning his programme in the
group.

Involvement of parents

The nature and amount of contact with parents varied substantially
from school to school. When asked whether parents were informed of

their child's admission to the group, the head of school C replied:

It's a moot point. This is why I like the in-school group. It's like moving a child to a different class, not like a special school [with all the formalities to go through]. I'd like the teacher in charge to make the contact verbally, but I wouldn't tell them formally.

Home visits were seldom made by the teacher in charge of school C's group. At school D, in contrast, all parents were consulted by means of a home visit from the teacher in charge before their child was admitted. At schools A and B the head or deputy interviewed parents at the school before admitting the child. The group teacher seldom, if ever, made home visits. Parents were notified at schools E and F, though the procedure varied from pupil to pupil. At both schools the teachers in charge were empowered to use their own discretion in deciding whether to make a home visit.

The whole question of teachers making home visits is, of course, controversial. The head of school F was happy for the teacher in charge of the group to make home visits, but not for any other teachers. He believed these were generally best left to the established support services such as education social work (known as education welfare in many LEAs) and the psychological service. On the other hand, the group teachers who did make regular home visits claimed to find these extremely helpful. The visits not only clarified the nature of the pupils' problems, but also secured the parents' active cooperation in what the group was trying to do for the child. The head of school B felt that this cooperation could be elicited more efficiently by means of an interview at the school, but the group at this school did not envisage the need for such active parent involvement in a rehabilitative programme as, for example, school D.

Observing the groups in progress

Introduction

Two members of the research team each spent a week observing the groups in progress, recording aspects of teacher–pupil interaction. School G was not included in this part of the study. As explained earlier, the group did not operate at all in the autumn term, and only contained one pupil in the week selected for systematic observation in the spring term of 1979. The technique used was event sampling. The research officer wore an ear-plug connected to a pocket tape recorder. She spent ten seconds observing what was taking place, followed by ten seconds recording on a set of sheets designed for the purpose. The signals to observe and record were a single and a double bleep respectively, pre-recorded on to the tape. Two observation schedules were used, alternating every eight minutes. One focused on a pupil's behaviour, and the other on the teacher's. In the case of pupil observations, each pupil was observed in turn. Observation took place throughout the school day, except in the lunch-hour, and mid-morning and mid-afternoon breaks. In addition there were a few occasions when systematic observation was impractical, for example on visits outside the school grounds.

A problem in this sort of study is the reliability of the observations. In other words, do two observers see the same things, and record them in the same way? Before starting the main part of the study, we spent a fortnight carrying out practice observations in two groups. By the end of this time a satisfactory reliability rate of 90 per cent had been achieved.

Teacher–pupil interaction

The first and most striking point about pupils' behaviour in all the groups was the high proportion of time spent working at the task set by the teacher. Table 7.5 shows only one group in which pupils were 'on task' (i.e. concentrating on an activity approved by the teacher) for less than 70 per cent of the observation periods. At school B, pupils were rated on task in a remarkable 96 per cent of observation periods. With the possible exceptions of schools D and F, the percentage of time on task was similar to the percentage reported in the behaviour modification literature after successful treatment (e.g. O'Leary and O'Leary 1979; Ward 1971).

It should not, of course, be thought that intense concentration on formal work was required for a pupil to be rated on task. He could be quietly working at a jigsaw, provided this was with the teacher's knowledge and approval. When not on task pupils were either daydreaming, doodling or on infrequent occasions being more overtly disruptive. Nevertheless, it is worth emphasising that we observed relatively little behaviour that could be termed disruptive. There were few incidents, in which the teacher seemed to be in any danger of losing control.

Table 5.5
Pupils' concentration in six special groups – per cent of observations

	School					
	A	B	C	D	E	F
Pupil recorded as 'on task'	79	96	83	69	82	73

One obvious explanation for the high percentage of on-task behaviour lies in the favourable teacher : pupil ratio noted earlier in the chapter. Another may lie in the fact that pupils were generally working alone on tasks which were well within their ability. Pupils in all six groups spent over 50 per cent of their time working on their own, with no direct contact with other pupils or with the teacher. We shall be discussing the curriculum shortly. At this stage it is worth noting that in all groups except one the majority of work was set by the group teacher on an individual basis. The exception was school C, where the group teacher taught all the pupils as a group.

The favourable teacher : pupil ratio and the fact that work could be set individually undoubtedly contributed to a stable atmosphere in most of the groups. Analysis of how the teachers spent their time in each group indicated that in all groups at least 40 per cent of the time was spent in direct contact with pupils. There were exceptions, but the majority of teachers did not simply set work, and spend the rest of the session marking or reading!

How was the high level of concentration in the groups maintained? One possibility is the systematic use of social reinforcement approval for 'good' behaviour and for work completed. Another is the teacher's immediate reactions to inappropriate behaviour, while providing pupils with alternative ways of behaving. In other words, if they are set educational tasks which interest them and are within their ability, pupils not only feel less need to behave in an unsatisfactory way, but also – especially in a closely supervised situation – have less opportunity. A further possibility is that removing a pupil to the special group removes him from the deviant subculture of his peers. As Hargreaves et al (1975) points out, pupils do not consistently behave in anti-social ways simply because teachers have labelled them as deviant. Another necessary condition is that this behaviour should elicit the approval and recognition of their like-minded peer group.

In the course of one week's observation in each group we recorded all instances in which teachers reprimanded a pupil or showed approval. The reprimand could be as mild as a sharply spoken 'Peter!' when the boy was not concentrating, or even the teacher clearing his throat in such a way as to draw the pupil's attention and make him stop what he was doing. Similarly, approval could be as little as an encouraging 'mm' in recognition of good work or a good reply. Yet although we adopted the most generous possible criteria in recording approval, Table 5.6 shows that we observed very little in any of the groups.

Perhaps the first point to make about Table 5.6 is that most classroom interaction studies show a higher rate of criticism for inappropriate behaviour than praise for desirable behaviour. Unfortu-

Table 5.6
Praise and criticism of pupils, expressed by teachers in six special groups – per cent of observations in which observed

	School					
	A	B	C	D	E	F
Teacher reprimands pupils (s)	2.3	0.3	0.9	3.3	3.4	1.2
Teacher praises/commends pupil(s)	1.2	0.4	0.5	1.1	0.9	0.9

nately, we were not able to distinguish between praise for good work and praise for good behaviour. The general trend towards low rates of positive reinforcement and higher rates of criticism is nevertheless consistent with the general trend in the research on classroom interaction.

Since the teacher's approval was clearly not the key to the generally stable behaviour of pupils in the groups, we must look for other explanations. Removal from a disruptive peer group and the size of the group itself have already been mentioned. We have also mentioned the fact that in most groups the majority of work was set by the teacher on an individual basis. It seems quite possible that the groups gave some pupils an unaccustomed experience of success. They were given work which was not too difficult for them; they had little choice about sitting quietly to work at it; and they could recognise their own achievement in completing it. This was particularly striking in school B's group. A similar explanation is that being placed in the group removed them from both the academic and social pressures of their ordinary classes, enabling them to concentrate better in a more relaxed atmosphere.

The curriculum
Table 5.7 shows the range of curriculum subjects provided in each group in the course of our week's formal observation. We can see that the groups differed widely in the breadth of the curriculum they appeared to provide. Thus, at school A only 15 per cent of the week was spent on English and maths, while at school F nearly half the week was spent on these subjects. The 'other activities' category includes a variety of things. At school A a substantial proportion of time allocated to other activities was spent on jigsaws. Talking, reading comics, or reading books not directly related to their English work accounted for most of the rest. Characteristically, school B allowed little time for such informal activities. No groups contained PE as a reg-

Table 5.7

Range of curriculum provided in each group in one week's observation – per cent of time

	School					
	A	B	C	D	E	F
English/maths	15	28	39	30	30	48
Other academic work	29	58	44	27	12	14
Art/craft	8	7	4	14	30	10
Other activities	48	7	13	29	28	28

ular timetabled subject, and only one was able to make occasional special arrangements for PE or similar activities. The scope for most forms of science was similarly restricted.

It certainly seemed to be the case that in a few groups the children were working to a somewhat restricted curriculum. There are, of course, arguments for this which will be dealt with in Chapter 6. A more immediate point, though, concerns the fact that most work was set by the group teachers. In theory, the head-teachers of all six schools expected that subject teachers would, when necessary, provide work for their pupils to complete in the special group. The rationale was, of course, that pupils needed to keep up to date with the work of the rest of their class if there was to be any hope of successful return. In practice, as Table 5.8 shows, we only saw substantial evidence of this happening in school B.

Two group teachers claimed they could obtain work from subject teachers when they needed it, but the general impression was one of considerable difficulty in establishing a close cooperative link over the curriculum between group teachers and their colleagues in the rest of the school. In the only school where this did seem to work successfully, school B, the teacher in charge of the group was given time specifically for the purpose of obtaining work from subject teachers.

Table 5.8

Amount of work set by subject teacher for pupil to complete while attending a special group

	School					
	A	B	C	D	E	F
Per cent of work set by subject teacher	0.9	38.3	2.9	3.4	0	2.0

Conclusions

Underlying assumptions
Besides the study of special groups, the research programme included
a study of exclusion and suspension from school, reported in Chapters
2 and 3, and an extensive investigation into unauthorised absence
from school, which is beyond the scope of this book. Altogether we
visited roughly three-quarters of the city's thirty-nine secondary
schools. Much of the discussion on these visits was informal, but at
least six head-teachers went out of their way to make the point that a
majority of disciplinary problems were created by aspects of the
school's own organisation. In one sense this is not surprising. Weak
teachers encourage disruptive behaviour, and most schools have their
fair share of weak teachers. Few head-teachers would deny this.

Yet most of the heads who emphasised the school's own contribution in disruptive behaviour went further than this. One made the telling, if not particularly original, point that if the curriculum was right
no child would consistently experience failure. In its literal sense,
remedial teaching is only needed because children have failed in their
ordinary classes. If the curriculum in the ordinary classes matches the
ability and interests of the pupils, then a situation can never arise in
which some pupils have to be withdrawn because of their failure to
cope. An idealistic view perhaps – but one which recognises the central importance of processes within the school in preventing – and
creating – problems. Returning briefly to the study of pupils suspended from school (Ch. 3), we wonder how often the intolerable
frustration of daily failure at school contributed to the provocative behaviour of these severely educationally retarded pupils.

Rehabilitation or prevention?
None of the heads of schools with special groups intended that the
groups should be used to deal with 'simple' problems arising, for example, from conflict with an inexperienced teacher. Moreover, with
the exception of school B, and possibly of school C, they all hoped
that the teacher in charge of the group would contribute actively to
the general level of understanding about problem children in the
school as a whole. The teachers in charge in at least two groups, in
schools D and E, spent much time and effort working with their colleagues in the mainstream, promoting greater understanding of difficult pupils, and working out programmes to maintain these children
in the mainstream, or return them to it.

Yet their essential model was nevertheless still a rehabilitative one.
An appropriate analogy is with an ambulance at the bottom of the

cliff, not with a wooden fence at the top. Perhaps inevitably, the emphasis was on reform or treatment rather than prevention. Just as the scope and aims of the curriculum have implications for remedial education, so the scope and aims of the school's pastoral and disciplinary networks have implications for special groups. There is an argument for remedial teachers focusing their attention on the ordinary curriculum, in order to present this curriculum in a way that suits the slow or retarded pupil. There is nothing revolutionary in this concept. It is at the heart of all mixed-ability teaching. If a child or group of children fail to make progress, the question is not so much what is wrong with the children as what is wrong with the methods used to teach them.

In practice these are not exclusive. Yet the special groups which we studied seemed to concentrate on the pupil more than on the context in which he had presented problems. No head-teacher seemed to see the group primarily as a way of giving staff and teachers a 'cooling-off period' which would allow a cool, careful look at the stresses in school or at home which had precipitated the problem and how these could be overcome. We shall argue shortly that most of the questions arising from our study of special groups arose either from failure to recognise this as the logical implications of their stated aims, or from failure to prepare pupils adequately for problems they would meet again on return to the mainstream.

Chapter 6

Special groups and suspension from school: uses, limitations and alternatives

Some questions arising from the study

Limitations in the study

Two limitations in our study of special groups should be repeated at this point. First it was carried out in three terms from the autumn term of 1978 to the summer term of 1979; over three-quarters of the information was gathered in the first two of these terms. Second the study was confined to Sheffield secondary schools, though it had the advantage of including *all* schools with special groups. Hence we cannot be certain how far the results also apply to special groups in other LEAs.

We nevertheless regard this as less of a problem in practice than it is in theory. If there is one consistent characteristic in the proliferation of special groups, it is that they have developed on an *ad hoc* basis. Local education authorities have encouraged them without imposing direction. The nature of the English education system makes this almost inevitable. The LEA can guide and advise, but it cannot easily direct; to do so strikes at the heart of the head-teacher's much-prized autonomy. In as controversial an area as disruptive behaviour, few LEAs will be prepared to tell head-teachers how they should run their groups. As special groups elsewhere have sprung up in the same *ad hoc* way as in Sheffield, similar questions are likely to arise. Moreover, we shall see shortly that these questions arise from their position within, and from their relationship to, the school as a whole. In other words, the key issues are not peculiar to Sheffield; they are inherent in any policy of basing a special group for disruptive pupils in an ordinary school.

The other limitation in our work – that most of the field-work took place in two terms of intensive study – raises more difficult questions. We thought it important to observe what the groups actually did rather than confine ourselves to the necessarily second-hand accounts of head-teachers and group teachers. This meant that we were able to make a number of factual statements about the groups *as we observed them*. The limitation lies in the changing nature of some of the groups. We saw in Chapter 5 how the original aims of groups in schools A, B and C had either been modified or extended. Yet changes also took place over much shorter periods of time. The number of pupils in each group, for example, varied from week to week, and in some schools from lesson to lesson, depending on how many pupils were attending part-time. In one or two groups, the curriculum too could vary from week to week, depending on the pupil's needs at the time.

There are two answers to these criticisms. First, only one teacher in charge of a group thought the week we selected for intensive observation was seriously atypical, though several others thought the week had been atypical in relatively minor ways. This group was in school G and contained only one pupil throughout our week of observation. We therefore have not reported the results for this group. The second answer is that focusing on events at one point in time is a useful way of highlighting some of the day-to-day issues in running special groups. A long-term view contains the danger of glossing over difficulties which need to be recognised if the group is to benefit the school as a whole and the pupils selected to attend it. A final point is that our methodology did not, of course, enable us to carry out long-term follow-up of pupils passing through the groups. This is a question which we shall discuss in greater detail later in the chapter.

The expense of special groups

Our results suggest that special groups were fairly cheap to run, but expensive to staff. With one exception, school G, head-teachers agreed that they should not be staffed by one teacher working on his own. It is worth repeating that school G's group had to close in the autumn term 1978 owing to the illness of the group teacher. As a specialist field, groups are particularly vulnerable to this sort of problem. Their vulnerability is enhanced when the teaching load is not spread between several staff, following the practice in schools B, C and E.

Only one teacher in charge of a group was paid a salary commensurate with that of a head of a major curriculum department. To some extent the salary of the teacher in charge is dictated by the group's aims and objectives. Unfortunately, this was not always recognised. The head of school A said: 'I don't envy him his job, because in the final analysis he's got sixty members in his department' – in other words, the whole teaching staff! The teacher concerned was paid a Scale II allowance, the lowest possible salary for a position carrying special responsibility. It was hoped that the teacher in charge of this group would negotiate with his colleagues the objectives in a pupil's admission to the group, and the circumstances of his return. Yet his position in the school's teacher hierarchy made it virtually impossible for him to do so.

If the group teacher is to play an active part in rehabilitating pupils he must not only have the *personality* to negotiate with colleagues who will sometimes be distinctly unenthusiastic about a disruptive pupil returning to their classes. He must also be seen to have the *authority* to negotiate with them, by virtue of his position within the school's hierarchy. The only alternative, adopted at school B, is for the head-teacher himself to exert extremely close personal control over all aspects of the group, so that requests for cooperation from the group teacher have the force of directives from the head himself.

The curriculum

Except in school B, with its strict policy on early return to ordinary lessons, the curriculum in the groups seldom seemed to bear much relationship to the curriculum the pupil would be following in his ordinary lessons. Obtaining work from subject teachers for pupils to complete while attending a group appeared to present considerable difficulties. One reason for this was suggested in the last section. Groups varied both in the breadth of the curriculum they offered and in its academic bias. As we saw in Chapter 5, pupils in one group spent a substantial part of their time doing jigsaws or copying cartoons. In another they spent almost their whole time following formal curriculum topics.

We noted in Chapter 5 that the head of school C was becoming doubtful about the feasibility of phased return to ordinary lessons. While his plans for return to ordinary lessons on a full-time basis, with no intermediate period of part-time attendance in the group, may be open to question, his suggestions for the curriculum are of considerable interest. He recognised the problem of integrating the group timetable with the pupil's ordinary lessons. The solution was to place responsibility for the curriculum in the hands of subject specialists, who would themselves teach part-time in the group. Thus, the maths specialist who taught the group would be responsible for ensuring that each pupil's work was closely enough related to his ordinary timetable to make return to ordinary lessons feasible. This model meant that teachers for the group would have to be selected as subject specialists, apart, of course, from the teacher in charge, who would have general oversight.

Social education

In one sense the curriculum in all seven groups had a clear academic orientation. There were substantial variations in the relative emphasis placed on the formal curriculum and on broader social educational or therapeutic aims. The head of school D felt it would often be inappropriate for pupils in the group to follow the timetable on which they had been failing prior to admission. Similarly, the teacher in charge of school F's group felt that a primary school approach, with its greater reliance on project work and discovery learning, was more appropriate for his pupils.

Nevertheless the bias, even in these groups, was academic in the sense that social education was implicit rather than explicit. None of the groups adopted the explicit social training and 'behavioural' problem-solving approaches which we described in Chapter 5. Some group teachers, notably the group teachers in schools D, E and F did consciously aim to help pupils cope with stressful situations, both at home and at school. Their methods however, were indirect. They preferred to use the relationship between teacher and pupil, sometimes supplemented by incidents arising from day-to-day interaction in the group, as the basis for social learning and personal growth. None of the group teachers adopted the systematic teaching methods of, for example, the Hungerford Centre (Lane 1977; Lane and Millar 1977) in which pupils would read mini-plays illustrating a 'good' and a 'bad' way of coping with a difficult situation.

Return to the mainstream

We have noted the differences between the groups in the length of pupils' full-time attendance. Returning briefly to Table 5.2, the period of full-time attendance ranged between three weeks in schools B, F and G, to nineteen weeks in school D. The figures are misleading, however, if it is thought that all pupils returned to ordinary lessons after a period in the group. They did not. Four of the twelve pupils in school C's group, for example, left it because they were suspended from school. In school A one pupil left because he was committed to care by the Juvenile Court, and another because he reached school-leaving age. At school B, where return to ordinary lessons was virtually automatic as a result of the head's avowed policy that 'thou shalt not be a terminal case', return to the group following further problems was common. The head recognised this, preferring that pupils return for a further spell in the group than that they remain in it long term at any one time. We shall see shortly that a substantial proportion who attended a group in the autumn term 1978 were unavailable for interview the following spring term, owing to truancy, suspension or committal to care.

The overall impression was one of considerable difficulty in the question of return to ordinary lessons. Although the head of school A felt that his group had helped to reduce the problem of disruptive behaviour, it also seemed possible that this group's gradual evolution into a long-term educational alternative for certain pupils resulted in part from the group teacher's difficulty in arranging their successful return to ordinary lessons. In all the groups, except school E, which only admitted pupils in their first three years of secondary education, older pupils presented more problems in this respect.

School attendance

An interesting characteristic of school F, was that fifteen of the twenty-six pupils had been present at school for less than 50 per cent of possible attendances in the twelve weeks prior to their admission. Their mean attendance in this period was 12 per cent. While they were timetabled to attend the group for at least half the week, their mean attendance rose to 31 per cent. Whether this is viewed as a moderate or a dramatic improvement may depend on one's perspective. Most pupils showed some improvement while attending the group, but only two attended as much as 75 per cent of the time, and even these two were unable to sustain their improvement for more than a term. It was not worth while calculating the attendance of pupils after discharge to ordinary lessons as only half of the original poor attenders were discharged to ordinary lessons for more than half their timetable.

At the other schools a history of poor attendance was sometimes a contributory reason for placement in the group but very seldom a primary one. Three pupils at school B's group had been present for an average of 24 per cent of possible attendances in the twelve weeks prior to admission. While timetabled to attend the group for at least half the week, their attendance improved to an average of 74 per cent. In the twelve weeks following discharge to attend ordinary lessons for over half their timetable it fell only slightly to 69 per cent. An important feature here may have been the elaborate reporting procedure on discharge from the group, as described in Chapter 5. A similarly encouraging pattern was observed in three pupils with poor attendance records before admission to school D's group. Two of these pupils were still attending extremely well on follow-up; the third ceased to attend school at all on discharge from the group. The overall impression from the limited data on school attendance which we were able to collect suggests that admission to a group could help some pupils establish a pattern of regular attendance. There were, however, considerable individual variations; the teachers in charge were clear that special groups were no panacea for attendance problems.

Special groups, deviant behaviour and suspension

The effect of special groups on suspension rates

The special groups in Sheffield secondary schools did not fulfil the hope of reducing the number of pupils suspended. We recorded from the LEA's records the number of pupils from each school who had been reported as suspended, or excluded for at least three weeks: (a) in the two years before the group opened; (b) in the first two years of the group's existence. We also recorded the number of pupils transferred to special schools for ESN(M) or maladjusted pupils in the same periods. The reason for this was to control for the possibility that some schools might refer pupils to special schools as an alternative to exclusion or suspension. The results are seen in Table 6.1. School G could not be included in the table, as its group opened before the LEA started to keep readily accessible records on exclusion and special school transfers.

The evidence in Table 6.1 is unequivocal. These special groups cannot be seen as a way of reducing the number of pupils whom the school might otherwise have felt obliged to exclude or suspend. Schools A, B, C and E had excluded or suspended a significant number of pupils before opening their group. They continued to do so. Schools D and F, both of which served extremely disadvantaged areas of the city, seldom excluded or suspended before opening their

Table 6.1

Exclusion or suspension and transfer to special education from schools with special groups

| | Number of pupils from school | | | | | |
	A	B	C	D	E	F
Suspended or excluded for at least 3 weeks in 2 years before the group opened	6	7	14	1	7	2
Suspended or excluded for at least 3 weeks in first 2 years of the group's existence	4	17	25	0	7	2
Transferred to special school for ESN(M) or maladjusted pupils in 2 years before the group opened.	3	3	2	3	5	2
Transferred to special school for ESN(M) or maladjusted pupils in first 2 years of the group's existence.	1	3	4	3	4	9

groups, and continued not to do so. Distinguishing indefinite suspensions from temporary, albeit relatively long-term, exclusions altered this picture only at school B. This school was unusual in the LEA for having relatively few suspensions in proportion to the exceptionally high rate of exclusion for at least three weeks. Table 6.1 indicates that its special group did not solve the problem of exclusion. It did, however, provide a convenient avenue through which excluded pupils might return to school.

Table 6.1 also shows that opening a special group was not associated with a drop in the number of pupils transferred to special schools. At school F the number of pupils moving to special schools increased noticeably in the first two years after the group opened. Analysis of these referrals, however, showed that almost all were children with medical and/or 'emotional' problems, often associated with persistent school refusal. Few presented overtly disruptive behaviour at school, though several did so at home. In other words, they were the same sort of pupils for whom the group was started in the first place.

School influences on behaviour
We noted in Chapter 2 that exclusion rates varied dramatically between the LEA's thirty-nine secondary schools. We also reported that this variation was not associated in any systematic way with differences in catchment area (Galloway et al. 1981a). In this respect exclusion differs from persistent absenteeism, which is strongly associated with social problems, notably poverty, in the catchment area. In Chapter 5 we pointed out that the decision to open a special group was not associated with problems arising from any one type of catchment area, nor with any readily identified set of policies within the school.

This evidence did not, however, provide any information as to whether schools with high exclusion rates experienced more serious problems from a minority of pupils than schools with low rates. Nor did it tell us whether these schools experienced problems from a higher proportion of pupils. Both these questions are, of course, as relevant to schools with special groups as to schools with high, or low exclusion rates.

The seven schools with special groups included two, schools B and C, which had consistently high exclusion and/or suspension rates. In addition, we interviewed teachers and pupils at three schools without groups, school H, I and J. One of these, school H, also had a high exclusion rate. Thus, we had access to information about three of the four schools with the highest exclusion rates in the city. Our sample also included two schools with groups, schools D and G, and one without, school J, which had excluded very few pupils indeed for as long as three weeks. None had excluded more than three pupils in the three years prior to our study. Thus, within our sample of ten schools selected for intensive study, we had three with exceptionally high exclusion rates, and three with exceptionally low exclusion rates.

An important point to note here is that the 'high exclusion' schools did not differ from the 'low exclusion' schools on catchment area variables. There were differences *within* each group. Each group, for example, contained one school with a majority of owner-occupied houses in the catchment area, and one with a relatively small proportion of owner-occupied houses. We were not, however, able to identify any important differences *between* the two groups.

We asked the head-teacher or a senior member of staff in the three 'high exclusion' schools about the background to ten consecutive cases of exclusion or suspension. We also asked about the incident which had precipitated the decision to exclude or suspend. At the same time we collected information from the 'low exclusion' schools about the ten pupils who had caused them the greatest management problems in the preceding two terms. These pupils had not, of course, been excluded or suspended. Our question was: 'Which pupils came closest to exclusion or suspension?' In this way we hoped to establish whether the 'low exclusion' schools did in fact experience less severe problems from their pupils, or whether they experienced the same problems as the 'high exclusion' schools, but contained these problems internally.

The results of this exercise suggested that 'high exclusion' schools were likely to resort to exclusion or suspension for offences which would be dealt with differently at the 'low exclusion' schools. Thus, refusal to accept corporal punishment would automatically be followed by exclusion at school B, whereas school D would either find an alternative penalty, or contain the pupil under the direct supervision of a member of staff until he accepted it. Similarly, school C suspended at least two fifth-year pupils for persistent truancy, and two for defacing an exam paper. Schools D, G and J made clear that if a fifth-year pupil continued to truant after they had done everything in their power to secure his return, they might quietly turn a blind eye. They did not always adopt a low profile towards disruptions within the school, but explained that they regarded these as an internal matter, which should not be allowed to escalate to the point of long-term exclusion.

Each of the three 'low exclusion' schools reported two or three pupils who had presented very severe management problems. It seemed to us that the pupils concerned would almost certainly have been excluded or suspended had they behaved in the same way at schools B, C or H. On the other hand, teachers at the 'low exclusion' schools appeared to have considerable difficulty in recalling other pupils who had presented serious problems in the preceding term. In each case, they ended up by telling us about pupils who were already being considered for special education on account of learning difficulties with associated 'emotional' problems. The descriptions suggested strongly that these pupils would also have been strong candidates for special education had they attended a 'high exclusion' school.

Formal comparisons are not possible in this sort of survey; we can do no more than indicate the probable behaviour patterns behind high or low exclusion rates. Head-teachers' reports nevertheless suggest:

(a) that 'high exclusion' schools resort to this sanction following incidents which 'low exclusion' schools might contain internally;

(b) that 'high exclusion' schools experience serious problems from a larger proportion of their pupils than 'low exclusion' schools;

(c) that 'low exclusion' schools do experience severe management problems from a very small number of pupils, but are generally able to contain these pupils internally.

The method of containment varied. School G used its special group, while school D seemed to find close supervision by senior staff more appropriate for some pupils than the special group. With no special group, school J relied on senior staff, usually acting in very close liaison with parents.

Returning to special groups, we have already made clear that concern about the number of disruptive pupils in the school was an important reason for opening several of the groups. It does not, however, follow that schools which opened groups experienced more problems, let alone more severe problems, from their pupils than schools which did not. As we saw in Chapter 5, the reasons for opening a group varied from school to school. Interviews with the heads and senior staff in 'high exclusion' and 'low exclusion' schools merely confirmed these differences.

Pupils' perception of special groups

The 'hidden witnesses' *

We have noted that special groups varied in their underlying aims and in their specific objectives. We have also identified a number of apparent obstacles which make it difficult for them to achieve these objec-

---

* We are indebted for this term to Mr Rae Munroe of Auckland Teachers' College.

tives. The 'hidden witnesses' in much educational research are the pupils themselves – 'hidden' in the sense that their views and experiences are often overlooked. We interviewed pupils who had attended each of the seven groups in the autumn term of 1978. (In the case of school G, we interviewed pupils who attended the group during the spring term 1979. The group was closed in the preceding autumn term.) We were not able to trace all the pupils. Some had been committed to care, others were truanting, others had been suspended and at school B over a third of parents withheld permission for their child to be interviewed. Altogether we were only able to interview 55 per cent of pupils who had spent at least part of the autumn term attending a special group. Their comments are nevertheless revealing.

Reasons for admission

Few pupils were articulate about the reasons for their admission to the group. A group's aims were sometimes perceived in conflicting ways. Thus, one boy at school C told us how he had explained it to his parents:

'Well, I told them, it's sort of, like for bad boys, sort of keeping you away from the other lads. The teacher – him being the strictest in the school – he'll make you do the work.'

In contrast, another boy at the same school insisted:

'It wasn't a punishment. I'd fallen behind with my work, and it was to give me a chance to catch up.'

The pupils at schools E, F, D and G explained their entry to their group in terms of disruptive or non-conforming behaviour, for example, 'wagging it' (i.e. truancy), 'messing about . . . not working for one teacher'. Almost without exception, however, they insisted that they had been placed in the group in order to receive extra help, not as a punishment. Two pupils did think teachers in the mainstream of the school looked on the group as a punishment; the pupils themselves, though, made clear that they were glad to be in the group. This distinction was also made by pupils at school A's group. At school B, on the other hand, the pupils recognised that they had been placed in the group because of bad behaviour in ordinary classes but were less enthusiastic about remaining there.

Attitude to group

Very few pupils expressed hostility towards the group. This was true even in school B, whose group was the most highly structured, with the most explicit emphasis on hard work and good behaviour. The incentive to return to ordinary classes was not provided by this emphasis on hard work and good behaviour, but rather by the restriction on liberty in the lunch-hour and breaks. A girl summed it up like this:

I liked it in a way because it were quiet and I could get on with my
work. But it were in the breaks I didn't like it, when we just had to
sit in the room or walk around the tennis courts. Teachers even
took you to the toilet. But they do treat you better [in the group]
than they do in the classrooms. They did give you more help.

Teachers might have had mixed feelings about some pupils' enthusiasm for the group. An inveterate truant at school C (who, like the
girl just quoted was later suspended from school) told us:

The teacher in charge – he's one of the best teachers in the school.
I went everyday when I was in the group. The head used to think it
were torture, but the kids thought it were great – they used to do
something wrong to get in! All you had to do was stand outside the
school having a fag, and you'd get put in group. If you weren't
always in trouble, you would get stick, but if you were always in
trouble, like me, you'd go in group!

This boy was one of a group of fifth-year pupils at school C who had
consciously rejected the school's values. He and his peers felt that
their rejection was legitimised by the school's refusal to allow them to
attempt any external examinations. For this boy, placement in the
group merely confirmed his status in a deviant subculture.

Several pupils mentioned the teacher in charge of the group as an
important figure in their lives. A girl at school G said:

I can get on with my work better; and I like the teacher. I think
he's one of the best people I've known . . . . I told him my troubles,
and he helped sort them out.

Similarly, a pupil at School F said he only came to school at all in
order to talk to the group's teacher. A girl in the same group said:

He's one of the best teachers I've had . . . he'll sort out problems in
school for you.

The small number of pupils in the group and the consequent
opportunity for a teacher's attention was appreciated by many pupils.
On the other hand, they were critical of groups in which they felt the
curriculum was insufficiently demanding. One pupil at school A
admitted he had only resumed regular attendance because of the educational – and personal – help he received from the teacher, but others
seemed to want more of a challenge:

It were a laugh, but it did get boring after a bit.

Another pupil, this time at school C said:

It was all right, but boring. I was glad to get back in ordinary
school. I did less work in the group.

Few pupils admitted that the group helped them to cope with
stress at home. An exception was school D's group, whose teacher

made frequent home visits. One boy implicity acknowledged this link between home and school in two comments. The first was that the teacher helped him sort out problems in his family. The second was that if he 'messed about' in school, the teacher would tell his dad, and it wasn't worth the risk!

Pupils' perception of their own progress

When asked what effect they thought being with the group had had on them, pupils' replies fell into three broad categories. One set of replies emphasised the group's therapeutic role in helping them cope with stress at school, or less frequently, at home. A second set emphasised that they behaved better while attending the group, but denied that this improvement extended beyond the group. The third set of replies denied that the group had influenced them in any way. Quotations illustrate each sort of reply.

At first a girl at school G seemed a bit uncertain about the group's effect on her, but then elaborated:

It doesn't seem to be having any effect – except making me
happier. Mum says I seem to want to come to school now ... [and]
she's noticed I've gone home from school a lot happier. I seem to
get on with mum and dad better.

More cautiously, a thirteen-year-old boy at school E said:

I think I've changed a bit. I don't run around in class or answer
back so much .... It's not a punishment – it's a way of telling you
what is right and what's wrong.

Seven of the nine pupils we interviewed from school D thought the group had helped them. One said: When I first came I wouldn't go near lessons. Now I don't mind ...

[the group has] made a lot of difference. I don't wag it or argue
with teachers any more. I accept school more.

Helping pupils to behave in an acceptable way in a special group is a worthwhile aim in itself. Yet one also hopes that improvement will be reflected in similar change in the pupil's behaviour outside the group. Unfortunately, many of the pupils themselves were in no doubt that this did not happen. At school B a girl remarked:

The group brought me back to myself a bit – quietened me down –
until I got out .... I was being quiet until I got out.

She was subsequently suspended. At school C a boy, who was also suspended a few weeks later, made the same point. A boy at school D, where most pupils thought they had benefited from the group, said dryly on the subject of his return to ordinary lessons:

It made no difference to me; I carried on behaving the same as
before I went in [the group].

114

A few pupils denied that the group had made any difference to them. At school E a thirteen-year-old in the care of the local authority remarked, somewhat pathetically:

They tried to help, but it hasn't worked!

A sixteen-year-old at school C was even blunter:

I'd say no effect at all – none at all. It were just like an ordinary lesson.

As the interview took place shortly after his suspension for disobedience to one of the group's teachers, this was doubtless a truthful statement – from every point of view!

Return to ordinary lessons

Pupils at schools A, B and C admitted to difficulty in returning to ordinary lessons after a period in the group. A few pupils mentioned educational problems:

The others had gone further in front, and I was having to catch up all the time . . . . I wasn't given the right work to do when I was in the group.

As we observed this boy spending a large part of each day in the group doing jigsaws or copying comics, we could understand his problem. A more common difficulty, though, lay in the pupils' perceptions of their teacher's attitudes when they returned to ordinary lessons:

They just hold it against you – you having been in the group . . . .

They used to say: 'If you don't get on with your work, I'll send you back to the group.'

They expected me to play up, with me having been in the group.

They picked on me because I'd been in the group.

Conclusions

It would be as wrong to place too much emphasis on these pupils' accounts of their experiences in the groups as it would be to ignore them altogether. The sample of pupils was probably a biased one. As we have already noted, only 55 per cent of pupils who had spent part of the autumn term in the group could be traced, and obtained parental consent for an interview with us, when we returned to the schools in the spring term. Over two-thirds of the remaining 45 per cent were repeatedly absent, or had been suspended. (Even so, the 55% whom we did interview included four suspended pupils.)

Yet the pupils' accounts confirmed many of our own observations. The ostensibly strict discipline and work ethic of the groups in schools B and C did not appear particularly aversive to the pupils. On the other hand, many of the pupils themselves doubted whether the group's influence would extend beyond the group's own classroom.

The danger of informally labelling children as disruptive, so that they subsequently live down to a teacher's expectations, was discussed in Chapter 4. Pupils from at least three groups were quite conscious of this process. The value of close school–home cooperation was clear from the interviews with pupils in school D. These pupils also saw the group as a sanctuary which could support them, and in certain cases help them to retreat, when they faced stress in the school's mainstream. The same was true though less consistently, in schools E, F and G. The teacher in charge of school A's group was trusted as a counsellor – he was the only adult one girl felt able to tell that she was pregnant – but was not seen as a source of support in problems with teachers outside the group. Some pupils at schools B and C seemed to think a period in the group had had some deterrent effect, but none seemed to regard the group as a positive influence in helping them to learn new, socially more acceptable ways of behaving. This, of course, raises fundamental questions about the nature of disruptive behaviour, and the aims of therapeutic work.

Effect of special groups on teachers' perceptions

An important reason for establishing at least three of the Sheffield special groups was to enable ordinary teaching to continue without disturbance from a disruptive minority. This aim implies that we should attempt to assess the groups' impact on teachers and classes from whom the disruptive minority is removed. The methodological difficulties in this sort of assessment are virtually insuperable. It would theoretically be desirable to observe the class before the pupil's removal, again while he was in the group, and again on his return. And that would only tell us about the effect of one pupil! Inevitably, we compromised.

As part of a wider inquiry into aspects of discipline and pastoral care, we interviewed teachers in each of the ten schools selected for intensive study. We saw the teachers with special responsibility for pastoral care, and a random sample of the remainder. Altogether we interviewed 25–35 per cent of teachers in each school. In the course of the interview with teachers at schools with groups, we asked whether a pupil had ever been removed from their class in order to attend a group. When the reply was yes, we then asked whether, in the teacher's own experience, attending the group had benefited the pupil concerned. We also asked whether the teacher felt he himself had benefited from the pupil's removal, for example by a reduction in disruptive behaviour and associated tension in his class. Finally, we asked whether he had noticed any benefit to the remaining pupils. For example, was their behaviour or educational progress noticeably different following the removal of one or more pupils to the group?

Table 6.2 shows the number of teachers interviewed at each school who told us that at least one pupil had been removed from one of their classes in order to attend the group. Table 6.3 shows the number of teachers who thought the group benefited the children selected to attend it, and/or the teacher himself, and/or the rest of the class.

Table 6.2
Number of teachers from whose class a pupil had been removed in order to attend a special group

	School, and number of teachers interviewed						
	A N = 14	B N = 13	C N = 15	D N = 18	E N = 17	F N = 12	G N = 24
Per cent of teachers interviewed from whose class a pupil had been removed in order to attend a special group (%)	79	62	80	56	41	67	58

Table 6.3
Views of teachers, from whose classes a pupil had been removed in order to attend a special group, on the value of the group

	School, and number of teachers from whose classes a pupil had been removed						
	A N = 11	B N = 8	C N = 12	D N = 10	E N = 7	F N = 8	G N = 14
% of teachers who thought group benefited pupils selected to attend it	27	88	42	60	86	100	71
% of teachers who thought teacher benefited from pupil's transfer to group	64	63	33	50	0	63	43
% of teachers who thought remainder of class benefited from pupil's removal	64	38	83	60	57	50	86

A relatively small proportion of teachers at school E reported that a pupil had been removed from their class in order to attend the group. This reflects the limited age-range for which the group catered. The same applied to a lesser extent with schools D and G. A more important point, made by many teachers at all seven schools, was that they had not themselves requested the pupil's removal. The decision had been made on a higher level, often following disruptive behaviour outside the classroom.

The results shown in Table 6.3 are based on small samples and should be interpreted with caution. They contain a number of apparent inconsistencies. These seem less surprising, however, in the light of the teachers' other comments in the course of the interview. Only 27 per cent of the teachers with experience of pupils in school A's group, and 42 per cent in the case of school C's group, thought the group had benefited the pupils concerned. The explanation seemed to lie partly in their perception of the pupils as 'hopeless cases' or 'bad 'uns', and partly in poor liaison between the group and the mainstream, over the questions both of admission and of discharge from the group. The teachers we interviewed did not seem to feel that they were a part of this process. Consequently, they saw no reason to review their original assessment of the pupils. As we saw earlier in the chapter, this negative assessment was communicated to the pupils themselves, several of whom proceeded to give it apparent validity by continued truancy or by further disruption resulting in suspension.

At school B, in contrast, teachers were closely involved both in the pupil's progress while attending the group – they had to set appropriate work for completion in the group – and in his subsequent rehabilitation, through the daily report system. This seemed to focus their attention on positive aspects of the pupil's work and behaviour. At schools E and F something different seemed to be happening. Teachers in these schools did not, on the whole, regard pupils selected for the group as disruptive deviants. Rather, they were looked on either as inadequate children who needed support, or as 'nutters' who really should not be in an ordinary school. In either case, treatment was indicated rather than punishment, and they felt that the group had helped the children concerned.

We were at first puzzled by the discrepancy in schools C and E between the small number of teachers who told us that they personally had derived benefit from a pupil's placement in the group, and the much larger number who thought that the rest of the pupils in the class had benefited. If the latter was true, then surely the teachers themselves should also have felt some benefit. The explanation seemed to lie in the teacher's morale and level of job satisfaction.

Whether or not a teacher derives personal satisfaction or benefit from observing improved behaviour in the majority of pupils depends at least partly on her original objectives, and on her commitment to her colleagues and to the school as a whole. If she feels that high standards are unrealistic in classes of less able pupils, or that achievements with these pupils will not be valued by colleagues, then she is unlikely to feel greatly encouraged by a moderate change in the pupils' behaviour. The feeling of these teachers seemed to be that they could teach their classes, whether or not they were well behaved, and whether or not the school had a group. If the majority became more cooperative following a pupil's removal to the group, so much the better – but this was not going to affect their teaching. The pupils could learn if they wanted to.

Opposition to special groups

We have already made clear that some head-teachers were opposed in principle to the idea of setting up a special group. Our discussion of special groups so far has concentrated on the practical difficulties in running a special group successfully, rather than the, perhaps more theoretical, objections to having one in the first place. It may be useful now to look at these objections in more detail.

The head of school H had experimented with the idea of a special group in the past, but had abandoned it. His reasons were pragmatic rather than philosophical. In fact, he still regarded the principle of having a group as consistent with his philosophy for comprehensive school education; it was set up to meet the special needs of individual pupils. One reason for closing the group was that disruptive behaviour no longer presented such a challenge to the smooth running of the school:

'I think that now I don't see a group as necessary. We have a lower proportion of potentially difficult pupils than we did have, and as a comprehensive school staff we are more experienced. When we started there were only me and two others who had ever taught in a comprehensive school.'

Nevertheless, school H did still have problems with some of its pupils. Only three other secondary schools in the LEA reported as many exclusions or suspensions. A more important factor in the head's decision to abandon the group was:

. . . a feeling that the group was out of step with what most of the teachers were trying to achieve. There was a *feeling* that some of the group pupils were stirring up the others . . . they weren't

119

anti-school, just pro-group . . . and it seemed to make one or two pupils dependent on it so they couldn't leave it and we couldn't use it for anyone else. And there was a general view that [the pupils] didn't do very much in the group and weren't much less difficult at breaks and lunch times.

In other words, the problem was partly that other pupils were being encouraged to join the group, but mainly that the group constituted a potentially divisive anomaly with aims which were inconsistent with those of teachers in the main body of the school.

Both these problems were familiar to head-teachers of schools with groups. The head of school C told us of an occasion when notices had appeared around the school, claiming that: 'Group rules, OK!' Membership of a group can give pupils security, stability and a sense of identity. Unfortunately, as the head of school C pointed out, a sense of belonging can be harmful if it creates a commitment to values which are inconsistent with those of the school as a whole.

School B had anticipated this problem in three ways. First, the regime in the group was so tightly structured, with such close supervision, that pupils had little opportunity for deviant behaviour while attending the group. Second, they spent too short a period in the group to allow a group identity to establish itself. Finally, the curriculum in the group was closely related to the pupils' ordinary curriculum thus reducing the opportunity for pupils to feel that they were different, and had special status.

The head of school I cited a variety of Parkinson's law as a reason for not establishing a group:

We felt that if we created a special group – withdrawing children from lessons – we would really be saying that we didn't trust our colleagues. The senior staff all felt that if we created a group there would be a move to fill it. The group would cater for children who had fallen foul of teachers with the least patience and sympathy. The least successful teachers would need to use the group most.

In other words, setting up a group was seen as an admission that certain staff could not cope without extra help; this would implicitly legitimise their need for extra help.

Nevertheless, school I's head-teacher was not unsympathetic to the problems facing his less experienced colleagues. He continued:

But I'm afraid, if we can't give support to teachers who are doing the best they can in the classroom, then it may well be that we are forced to withdraw a few individuals from the normal class – simply because we can't give the classroom teachers the level of support they are entitled to demand. It seems to me the ideal is to have a senior teacher who can go into normal classes and give regular support to teachers who are having difficulties in coping – rather than withdrawing pupils from the natural class.

The head of school I had, in fact, submitted a request to the LEA for help in establishing this sort of support. It seemed a constructive and imaginative alternative to the idea of setting up a special group. He told us that the response from the LEA had been discouraging, but he had been advised informally that a request for help in setting up a special group might be more favourably considered. He remained reluctant to accept this advice:

My main argument against special groups is that . . . if you put youngsters into one it seems to me almost inevitable that they leave a vacancy for the role they played in the ordinary class. So someone steps in to fill the vacancy, and you are increasing the problems instead of reducing them; and the real pressures in this school are peer-group pressures. If the vast majority of youngsters accept the norm for relationships, it is very difficult for anyone to disrupt. Removing them to a special group is removing them from the most powerful pressure to conform.

We asked senior staff in schools with groups how they reacted to this argument. Some accepted it, but others dismissed as naïve wishful thinking the idea that the pro-social majority constituted the most powerful pressure to conform. It is worth pointing out, though, that school I served a disadvantaged catchment area, consisting principally of council semi-detached houses. In a 1973 survey it had the highest rate of persistent unauthorised absentees in the LEA. In the next three years the number of persistent absentees was reduced by more than half – a greater reduction than any other school in the city. The improved attendance, moreover, seemed to be matched by a similar change in the pupils' behaviour and in their attitudes towards the school. The head-teacher's claim about the power of a pro-social pressure group seemed to receive support from independent observations.

This argument was also put forward by the head of school J, who considered groups 'totally unnecessary'. Pointing out that disruptive children, like all children, learned from each other, he argued:

This is a cardinal problem in the whole issue . . . as soon as you identify children in this way they live down to your expectations. It's collecting all of your troubles into one area, and it's entirely negative. In simplistic terms, I'd rather divide than conquer.

Removing a pupil into a special group did not, he felt, remove difficulties from the bottom end of the academic or behavioural continuum.

It merely adds another dimension. You've still got the youngsters who have got academic difficulties, home difficulties and so on.

The real need, according to the head of school J, was for all pupils to know that a teacher would deal with their problems individually, identifying their strengths as well as their weaknesses. What he seemed to be claiming was that the school's pastoral care network should cater for all pupils, thus removing the need for a safety net to pick up the failures. This raises interesting questions about the organisations of pastoral care. These need to be dealt with as part of a wider discussion of discipline and pastoral care in the schools we studied.

Discipline and pastoral care: implications for policy and practice

Introduction

We have noted clear evidence that the wide variation between secondary schools in their exclusion rates is not associated in any obvious way with differences in their catchment areas. Although we lack conclusive evidence, it seems likely both that 'high exclusion' schools resort to exclusion more readily than 'low exclusion' schools, and also that they experience severe problems from a larger number of pupils. We have also noted that secondary school heads vary in their attitudes towards special groups. Here, too, the variation appears unrelated to variables in the school's catchment area. Neither special groups nor exclusion can usefully be studied in isolation. Both must be seen in the wider educational context of the school concerned.

While a detailed sociological analysis of each school clearly lay beyond our scope, we did interview random samples of pupils in each school about aspects of their school's discipline and pastoral care. In selecting pupils for interview we identified at random 12 per cent of pupils in two age-groups: fifteen- to sixteen-year-olds in their final year of compulsory education, and eleven- to twelve-year-olds. Most of the latter were in their first year of secondary schooling, having transferred to secondary school from a middle school at the age of twelve. A minority were in their second year, having transferred from a junior school at eleven. Although we originally identified 12 per cent of pupils in each age-group, the number we actually interviewed at each school varied between 8 and 12 per cent. This depended on the numbers who were ill or truanting. In addition, a few parents refused permission for us to interview their children.

Our aim was to complement the information we had already received from interviews with head-teachers and with a random sample of teachers throughout the school. More specifically, we hoped to consider the pupil's experiences of discipline and pastoral care, and see whether these shed further light either on their school's policy towards special groups, or on their school's use of exclusion or suspension.

Possible alternative sanctions

A critical question about special groups is whether they are set up as an alternative to other, perhaps less desirable sanctions. There is little doubt, for example, that the Inner London Education Authority's policy of encouraging behavioural units is motivated at least partly by a desire to assist teachers in phasing out corporal punishment. None of the Sheffield groups were set up with this objective. We nevertheless thought it would be interesting to see what sanctions were routinely used in the ten schools we studied. Moreover, there was no doubt that six of the seven groups were set up at least partly because of concern that traditional sanctions were proving unsuccessful with a number of disruptive pupils. The exception of course, was school F, which catered mainly for pupils with emotional or family problems. We wondered whether the groups were replacing these traditional sanctions, or whether the groups were being used when they had failed. If the former was the case, one might expect to find higher rates of traditional punishments in schools which had no groups.

Similar questions can be asked about exclusion or suspension. We wondered whether these procedures were used in preference to more traditional sanctions such as corporal punishment. If so, we might expect to find low rates of corporal punishment in schools with high exclusion rates, and vice versa.

Table 6.4 shows the number of pupils at schools with groups and schools without groups who told us that they had received corporal punishment within the last twelve months, or been placed in detention in the same period. Table 6.5 gives the same information about schools with high and low exclusions rates. Two points need to be made about the information in these tables. First, the LEA's regulations state that corporal punishment must be recorded in the school's punishment book and administered by a teacher with at least four years' experience, in the presence of a witness. We deliberately did not distinguish between formal corporal punishment, administered strictly in accordance with the LEA's regulations, and informal corporal punishment which was not officially recorded, nor administered in the presence of a witness. A number of head-teachers expressed reservations about our figures, as they indicated that more pupils had received corporal punishment than were shown in the school's official punishment book as having received it. They suggested that some pupils might have

Table 6.4
Use of corporal punishment and detention, as reported by random sample of pupils: (I) Schools with and without special groups

School and number of pupils interviewed	Schools with special group														Schools with no special groups					
	A		B		C		D		E		F		G		H		I		J	
	(m)	(f)	(m)	(f)	(m)	(f)	(m)	(f)	(m)	(f)	(m)	(f)	(m)	(f)	(m)	(f)	(m)	(f)	(m)	(f)
	24	22	33	41	21	22	40	52	30	22	33	30	36	44	38	29	28	31	35	17
Boys who said they had received corporal punishment in the last 12 months (15–16-year-olds) or since admission (12–13-year-olds) (%)	50		18		19		25		7		48		14		13		4		29	
Girls who said they had received corporal punishment in the last 12 months (15–16-year-olds) or since admission (12–13-year-olds) (%)	9		12		0		17		0		10		0		0		3		0	
Boys and girls who said they had been placed in detention in the last 12 months (15–16-year-olds) or since admission (12–13-year-olds) (%)	33		53		67		40		29		10		35		49		81		75	

Table 6.5
Use of corporal punishment and detention, as reported by random sample of pupils: (II)
Schools with high and low exclusion rates

	School and number of pupils interviewed					
	Schools with high exclusion rates			Schools with low exclusion rates		
	B	C	H	D	G	J
	(m)(f)	(m)(f)	(m)(f)	(m)(f)	(m)(f)	(m)(f)
	33 41	21 22	38 29	40 52	36 44	35 17
Boys who said they had received corporal punishment in the last 12 months (15–16–year-olds) or since admission (12–13-year-olds) (%)	18	19	13	25	14	29
Girls who said they had received corporal punishment in the last 12 months (15–16–year-olds) or since admission (12–13-year-olds) (%)	12	0	0	17	0	0
Boys and girls who said they had been placed in detention in the last 12 months (15–16–year-olds) or since admission (12–13-year-olds) (%)	53	67	49	40	35	75

claimed to have been hit or caned in order to appear 'tough' or demonstrate 'machismo'. We cannot, of course, *prove* that this did not happen. Nevertheless the pattern of responses from different schools suggests that it was unlikely. It was not the case, for example, that in each school more older boys consistently reported having received corporal punishment than younger ones. Moreover, most of the pupils were able to be quite specific about the incident, again indicating that it was not fabricated on the spur of the moment. The second point about Tables 6.4 and 6.5 is that many pupils said their whole class had been placed in detention, either for unsatisfactory work or for unsatisfactory behaviour. We were not able to distinguish between pupils who were placed in detention because they were members of a particular class, and pupils who had been given detention for more specifically individual reasons.

With these provisos, Table 6.4 offers little support for the view that special groups were being used as an alternative to corporal punishment, nor for the view that schools without groups might have higher rates of corporal punishment. This table, together with our interviews with teachers in charge of groups, and with special group pupils themselves, suggests that corporal punishment was still used on a significant minority of pupils. It seems to be the case, except in school F, whose group did not cater primarily for overtly disruptive pupils, that groups were used when traditional sanctions had failed.

Two schools with no group, H and I, had exceptionally infrequent reported use of corporal punishment. On the other hand, school I, where corporal punishment occurred very seldom indeed, and school J, where it occurred more often, made exceptionally frequent use of detention. Analysis of the interviews indicated that a majority of pupils had been placed in detention as members of a class, rather than for individual offences. In many cases the detention had lasted for as little as ten minutes, while the class completed extra work before being released for the lunch-hour.

Table 6.5 provides rather modest support for the view that schools with high exclusion rates used corporal punishment less frequently than schools with low rates. More pupils in two of the latter group of schools said they had received this form of punishment than in any of the 'high exclusion' schools. On the other hand, it is worth pointing out that we interviewed suspended pupils from schools B, C and H as part of the study of suspension from school reported in Chapter 3. *All* the boys we interviewed said they had received corporal punishment, and their head-teachers subsequently corroborated these statements. Hence, it appears that exclusion and suspension is not used as an alternative to corporal punishment at these schools, although there is some rather limited evidence that they administer this sanction to a smaller proportion of pupils than some schools which seldom exclude or suspend.

Pastoral care

Part of our motivation in interviewing a random sample of pupils in each school was to investigate the possibility of an association between the use of exclusion or suspension and the pupils' perceptions of the school's pastoral care system. More specifically, we wondered whether low exclusion rates reflected a favourable attitude towards the school's pastoral care network among pupils in the school as a whole. Conversely, would high exclusion rates reflect the reverse? A similar question could be asked with respect to special groups. We wanted to see whether the head's perceiving of a need for a special group was associated with a lack of confidence in the school's pastoral care network on the part of the pupil consumers.

We asked each pupil whether he, or she, thought that at least one teacher was interested in him as a individual, apart from a natural in-

Table 6.6
Pupils who thought at least one teacher took a personal interest in them, extending beyond their academic work: (I) Schools with and without special groups

Schools	11–12 year-old-pupils		15–16 year-old-pupils	
	Number interviewed	% giving positive reply	Number interviewed	% giving positive reply
With special groups				
A	26	54	20	55
B	35	46	39	62
C	22	45	21	48
D	46	52	46	70
E	28	25	24	80
F	32	44	31	74
G	31	42	49	63
With no special groups				
H	32	64	35	66
I	32	53	27	74
J	24	29	28	71

Table 6.7
Pupils who thought at least one teacher took a personal interest in them, extending beyond their academic work: (II) Schools with high and low exclusion rates

Schools	11–12 year-old-pupils		15–16 year-old-pupils	
	Number interviewed	% giving positive reply	Number interviewed	% giving positive reply
Schools with high exclusion rates				
B	35	46	39	62
C	22	45	21	48
H	32	64	35	66
Schools with low exclusion rates				
D	46	52	46	70
G	31	42	49	63
J	24	29	28	71

terest in the quality of his schoolwork. The results are shown in
Tables 6.6 and 6.7. They reveal interesting variations within schools
between eleven- to twelve-year-old pupils and fifteen- to sixteen-year-
olds. At schools E and J, for example, less than 30 per cent of eleven-
to twelve-year-olds answered this question positively. By the age of
fifteen to sixteen, over 70 per cent did so.

Table 6.6 provides only moderate evidence that pupils in schools
with special groups differed from pupils in schools with no groups in
the interest which they thought their teachers took in them. By the
final year of compulsory education, at least two-thirds of pupils in all
three schools without groups thought a teacher took a personal interest
in them. In schools with a group there was much greater variation.
It is of particular interest that the lowest percentages in fifteen- to sixteen-year-olds were at schools A, B and C. These of course, were the
three schools which originally set up their groups in order to cope
with severely disruptive pupils who might otherwise have been candidates for exclusion. The evidence suggests that a significant number of
pupils in these schools saw their teachers as uninterested in them as
individuals. The logical implication is that this perception, whether it
was correct or false, may have been associated with the problems
which led the schools to establish special groups. Nevertheless, this
suggestion must remain tentative. The number of pupils interviewed
was not large, nor were the differences between schools large enough
to warrant firm conclusions.

Table 6.7 shows the same tendency as Table 6.6. At two of the
three schools with exceptionally low exclusion rates, more fifth year
pupils thought a teacher was interested in them as individuals than at
any of the three schools with exceptionally high rates. The other 'low
exclusion' school, school G, was on a par with schools B and H in the
'high exclusion' group. While it is by no means conclusive, the
evidence suggests that schools with high exclusion rates may be less
successful than schools with low exclusion rates in persuading the
majority of pupils that teachers are interested in them. This seems
particularly to be the case with school C, where less than half the
pupils thought at least one teacher was interested in them as individuals.

Academic bias and organisation
The schools varied in their policies towards mixed ability teaching.
School I had introduced mixed-ability teaching for all age-groups be-
low the sixth form, in all subjects except maths. Others, such as

school B, preferred to band pupils into upper and lower ability groups. Others still taught some subjects in mixed-ability classes, but 'setted' pupils by ability for others. These variations were not, however, associated in any obvious way with the number of pupils excluded or suspended, nor with the decision to establish a special group.

We wondered whether the degree of academic pressure imposed on pupils might be associated with problems which resulted either in the decision to set up a group or in the decision to exclude or suspend. One measure of academic pressure is the amount of homework which the pupils are required to complete each evening. When we interviewed a random sample of pupils from each school, we asked them how long, on average, they spent on their homework each night. Again, there was great variation between schools. At schools B and H, less than 35 per cent of fifteen- to sixteen-year-olds spent over an hour. At schools E and J, over 70 per cent spent this long. Yet here, too, the variation was not related in any systematic way to the areas we were studying.

Two of the schools which seldom excluded or suspended pupils had incorporated a former selective school on the reorganisation of secondary education into a comprehensive system. The same applied to two of the schools with exceptionally high exclusion rates. Hence, the mere fact of incorporating a selective school, with the implicit possibility of retaining a selective school's policies and ethos, did not appear relevant. Nevertheless, the 1973 pilot study (Galloway 1976a) indicated that comprehensive schools which had incorporated a former selective school tended to exclude or suspend more pupils than those which had not. We wondered whether this fact could help to explain the high exclusion rates in schools B and H, both of which had incorporated a former selective school.

The two schools differed in a number of important ways, for example, their policy towards mixed-ability teaching, but there were some striking similarities. Both placed importance on wearing school uniform. Both placed a high priority on academic standards. Both could identify socio-culturally impoverished pockets of their catchment areas. The majority of pupils with learning and/or behaviour problems lived in these areas. Both expected – and generally achieved – high standards of behaviour. The trouble, of course, was that a few pupils could not or would not conform to these high standards. Most of the time the unsettled or educationally retarded pupils cooperated with the system. Occasionally, but inevitably, the uneasy truce broke into open confrontation. When this happened, exclusion or suspension was the likely result.

Conclusions and summary

At the start of this chapter we raised a number of questions which emerged from our study of special groups. We went on to report the results of interviews with pupils who had attended special groups, with teachers in the mainstream of the school, and with pupils in the mainstream of the school. We also looked at some of the practical and theoretical objections to special groups as described by head-teachers who doubt their usefulness. We used the results of these interviews to examine the association between a perceived need for a special group and the behaviour and attitudes which prevailed in the school as a whole. Three of our ten schools reported exceptionally high exclusion rates, while another three reported an exceptionally small number of pupils as excluded or suspended. We were therefore also able to use the results of interviews with pupils and teachers to look at the association between the use of exclusion or suspension, and the behaviour and attitudes which prevailed in the school as a whole.

It would be fair to say that none of our evidence is conclusive, except perhaps the figures in Table 6.1 which show that opening a special group is not associated with a drop in the number of pupils excluded or suspended. Yet it is also true that most of our evidence points towards the importance of school processes as critical variables both in the development and in the management of disruptive behaviour. We are not, of course, denying that pupils who were excluded or placed in special groups presented severe problems. In Chapter 3 we provided clear evidence that they constituted an exceptionally vulnerable and challenging group. Nor are we denying the importance of catchment area variables. We are simply asserting that processes within the school are also influential in determining the nature, the prevalence and the severity of disruptive behaviour.

In this respect the evidence from our study of seven schools with special groups and three with no groups is consistent with much of the sociological literature on deviance reported in Chapter 4. It is easy, for example, to see how some of the groups facilitated the development of 'secondary deviance', whereby the school's own response to disruptive behaviour had the effect of confirming a pupil's status in an anti-authority subgroup, or his self-image as a member of one. With hindsight, one can see a depressing inevitability in some pupils' progress. Having frequently been in trouble in the main body of the school, they were referred to the group; on return from the group they found teachers expecting further trouble because they had been in the group; further confrontation occurred, culminating in the ultimate accolade of suspension.

Our emphasis on school processes is also broadly consistent with the results of other comparative studies, such as those by Rutter et al. (1979). Earlier studies both in North America (Coleman et al. 1966) and in the UK (DES 1967) found no apparent association between structural variables such as a school's size or age of buildings, and various output measures such as educational progress. Our evidence on disruptive behaviour found a similar lack of association. However, what neither the Coleman nor the Plowden Reports would have predicted was our evidence that the school itself exerts an important influence both on its pupils' behaviour and on how they are dealt with when they behave in unacceptable ways.

Our evidence suggests that both disruptive behaviour and the school's response when disruptive behaviour occurs reflects the unwritten, and often unspoken attitudes and practices within schools. Together these attitudes and practices constitute the nebulous concepts of 'school ethos' or the school's 'hidden curriculum'. It is important not to misunderstand this point. Our emphasis on the school's importance as a social and educational organisation should be encouraging to teachers. It suggests that they can – and do – affect their pupils' behaviour. On the other hand, disruptive behaviour presents enormous problems in some schools, causing great stress to the teachers concerned. No teacher *seeks* stress of this kind, even though the school's policies and the teacher's own practices may contribute to it. The relationship between teacher stress and disruptive behaviour is a complex one, deserving a chapter to itself.

Chapter 7

Disruptive pupils and teacher stress

Introduction

To say that disruptive behaviour causes stress for teachers is platitudinous. If it did not cause them stress, they would not be worried about it. Yet the relationship between disruptive behaviour and teacher stress is a great deal more complex than this banal statement implies. As Dunham (1976) points out, stress can result from organisational decisions imposed on teachers by outside agencies, from role conflict or role ambiguity within the school, and from poor working conditions, as well as disruptive behaviour. The implication, recognised explicitly by Borland (1962), is that disruptive pupils can be *either the cause or the effect* of teacher stress.

It is not hard to see how family tensions may affect the quality of a person's teaching. (Pressures at school may, of course, have contributed to the family tensions in the first place, but let us overlook this possibility for the moment.) It is equally easy to see the possible connection between half-hearted teaching, pupils' boredom, and disruptive behaviour. To take an extreme example, how many people can concentrate on their work when their marriage is breaking up? In the same way, tensions within the staffroom can affect a teacher's confidence, lowering her morale and reducing both her energy for, and commitment to, the business of classroom teaching. To expect that this will not be reflected in the pupil's behaviour is unreasonable.

This chapter starts with a brief discussion of existing evidence about the nature and causes of teacher stress, with particular emphasis on the importance of pupils' behaviour. We then look at some teachers' accounts of disruptive incidents, and the ways in which these incidents were handled. We use these accounts to illustrate the circumstances in which disruptive behaviour becomes a source of serious stress. Finally, we review evidence from the Sheffield studies to show how the *potential* stress engendered by disruptive behaviour may be contained, so that it does not *actually* become acutely stressful.

What is teacher stress?

The question of definition
The term 'stress' can be defined in ten different ways by ten different
people. In popular use, stress usually implies a negative feeling, with
the implication that the person will be happier if the causes of stress
can be reduced. Yet stress can result from too little stimulation as well
as from too much. We saw in Chapter 6 how pupils attending at least
one special group complained of it being 'boring'. Moreover, there is
an argument that some stress is necessary for the satisfaction which results from high standards. Aiming at high standards implies the risk
of failure; the higher the person flies, the harder he can fall.

Dunham (1977) quotes Hebb's (1972) model in which a moderate
level of anxiety, or stress, can be stimulating and lead to improved
performance. An excessive level of anxiety, in contrast, is potentially
destructive as it can lead to over-reaction, confused thinking, panic and
exhaustion. An example which most teachers may recognise, both in
themselves and in their pupils, is the stress engendered by taking an
exam. Moderate stress in this situation helps the candidate to think
better and write faster. A few unfortunate individuals, in contrast, 'go
to pieces'. Their minds 'go blank', and they become incapable of recalling what they know.

Kyriacou and Sutcliffe (1978) distinguish two common uses of the
term 'stress'. The first is an 'engineering' model. Stress is seen as
pressure exerted by the environment, just as in engineering steel can
be stressed by external forces. In a teacher's case, pressure might be
exerted by factors such as poor working conditions or conflicting demands on her time. The second model is a physiological one, which
emphasises the individual teacher's perception of a condition as stressful. It is called a physiological model because early research used physiological measures to identify stress. Increased heart-rate, and the release of adrenalin into the bloodstream, for example, are immediate
physiological responses to stress. Medium-term responses may be increased susceptibility to minor illnesses such as colds, sore throats or
headaches. Long-term responses may be hypertension, peptic ulcer or
diabetes. Cobb and Rose (1973) showed that the last three were all unusually prevalent in one high-stress occupation, air-traffic controllers.

The physiological model does not, of course, overlook the importance of 'environmental' pressures such as poor working conditions. It
merely emphasises the importance of the way the individual teacher
perceives and reacts to these pressures. Kyriacou's and Sutcliffe's
(1979) own definition of stress deserves to be quoted in full in spite of
its technical wording:

Teacher stress may be defined as a response of negative effects (such as anger or depression) usually accompanied by potentially pathogenic physical changes (such as increased heart rate) resulting from aspects of the teacher's job and mediated by the perception that the demands made upon the teacher constitute a threat to his self-esteem or well-being, and by coping mechanisms activated to reduce the perceived threat.

There are two key parts to this definition. The first is: 'The perception that the demands made upon the teacher constitute a threat to his self-esteem or well-being.' In other words, whether a *potential* stress, such as disruptive behaviour, becomes *actually* stressful depends on whether the teacher perceives it as a threat to his self-esteem or well-being. If, for example, he is confident that he can cope with the problem himself, or that he can call in a colleague for help without any reduction in self-esteem, he is unlikely to experience stress. On the other hand, he will feel stress if either of the following apply:

(a) he feels he cannot cope with the demands made on him;
(b) he thinks he *could* cope with them, but feels that they conflict with his own higher-order values. An example of a 'higher-order' value is high academic standards, which might have to be sacrificed in order to cope with a disruptive pupil.

The other key part of the definition is the importance attached to 'coping mechanisms activated to reduce the perceived threat'. The point is that stress results when coping mechanisms fail to deal adequately with the problem. Kyriacou and Sutcliffe note Lazarus' (1967) argument that stress is 'the reflection or consequence of coping processes which attempt to reduce the threat'. Returning to disruptive pupils, their model implies that stress results from the teacher's failure to deal with the problem, and from consequent reduction in his self-esteem.

Some causes and effects

In a study of nineteen primary schools in Sheffield, Pratt (1978) found a relationship between financial hardship among pupils' parents and stress reported by teachers. Pratt's measure of financial hardship was the number of pupils receiving free school meals. He also found a tendency, particularly among teachers of deprived children, for stress to increase with the age of the pupils.

Pratt was not able to control for the possible effect of the teacher's age and experience. An earlier study of teachers' illnesses, however, had suggested that absence due to illness was most widespread in the early years of teaching (Simpson 1962). The assumption here is that absences due to illness may often reflect stress at work. Support for this view is provided by information which Dunham (1976) obtained from teachers attending in-service training courses. Simpson notes that in most other occupations the incidence of absence increases with age. This is not the case with teachers; indeed male teachers showed a noticeable drop in sickness rates in the 'promotion zone' of the twenty-five- to thirty-nine-year-old age-group.

Superficially it is easy to see why younger teachers might be under greater stress than their more experienced colleagues. They are still learning the art of teaching, and have not acquired the necessary coping strategies. These are needed as much for coping with noise levels or inadequate equipment as with disruptive pupils. This may be true, but is nevertheless based on a superficial assessment of the problem. In particular it underestimates the importance of the social psychology of the school.

Hargreaves (1978) drew a painfully perceptive caricature of what teaching can do to teachers. In so doing, he showed that a major source of stress *for* teachers may unwittingly be created *by* teachers. His argument started uncontroversially: 'The work people do leaves its mark on them. The culture of a profession... appears in the individual as a set of personality traits.' In his caricature, Hargreaves claims that teachers become didactic, 'talking, repetitiously, from lesson to lesson, term to term, year after year'. They also, he claimed, became petty, with an exaggerated need for rules and regulations.

Hargreaves half recognised that both the didacticism and the pettiness might be necessary coping strategies. Without social control, teaching is impossible. Unfortunately they also 'produce that distinctive, progressive *exhaustion* which is a major characteristic of teachers. Other professionals get tired; teachers become exhausted.' This exhaustion is made worse, Hargreaves claimed, by the lack of supportive relationships among teachers. The problem is twofold. Admitting that you have a problem feels like admitting that you are incompetent. At the same time, offering to help a colleague implies that you think she is incompetent. Each teacher is left to solve her own problems, presumably by a process of trial and error. 'Teachers bear their stress in painful isolation. It attacks the heart of the teacher, both physically and metaphorically.'

Hargreaves admitted that his picture was a caricature. Yet like all successful caricatures, it held more than a grain of truth. Teaching can be an extraordinarily lonely profession. The loneliness of the classroom is compounded by that of the staffroom. Disruptive behaviour is the most striking example of stress which too often has to be borne in painful isolation. For many teachers, admitting to bad classroom discipline is paramount to admitting that they are bad teachers.

135

The effects of disruptive behaviour

In a useful review of previous research on teacher stress, Kyriacou and Sutcliffe (1977) found that no major studies had identified maintaining classroom discipline as the most important source of teacher stress. On the other hand, other sources, such as Caspari's (1976) book, *Troublesome Children in Class*, were in no doubt about the stress engendered by difficult pupils.

Kyriacou and Sutcliffe acknowledged that research might have underestimated the importance of disruptive behaviour as a source of stress. Three possible reasons were:

(a) that teachers only report as stressful those aspects of their job which can be changed by administrative decision, such as low salary or large classes;

(b) that 'ego-defensiveness' leads to under-reporting of dissatisfactions which imply personal failure;

(c) that teachers themselves may not be fully aware of the stress engendered by the need to maintain classroom discipline.

The second two suggestions received some indirect support from a survey of probationary teachers (Gough 1974). These teachers identified teaching mixed-ability classes as their principal source of stress. Their head-teachers, however, considered classroom discipline the major teaching problem.

Borland's (1962) study in New Zealand illustrates some of the difficulties in assessing the influence of disruptive behaviour on teacher stress. He found that only 2.4 per cent of teachers had persistent worries over discipline problems, which interfered with their sleep, their efficiency as a teacher or their health. Only 2.6 per cent said they were caused 'serious worry' about maintaining the necessary discipline to carry on work. Yet although relatively small numbers admitted to this level of anxiety, nearly 17 per cent admitted to 'serious worry' over pupils' socially unacceptable behaviour.

In contrast, two recent American studies have reported disruptive behaviour as the greatest single cause of teacher stress. An investigation by the Chicago Teachers' Union (Cichon and Koff 1980) identified four clusters of stressful experiences. The first involved issues of 'priority' concern, such as dealing with problem children, being threatened with personal injury or being subjected to verbal abuse. The teachers surveyed reported these incidents as causing them greater stress then the themes of 'management tension', for example overcrowded classrooms, or 'doing a good job', for example teaching retarded pupils. Least stressful of all were 'pedagogical functions', such as discussing children's problems with parents or taking extra course work for promotion. These results were broadly similar to another

American study in New York (Anon 1980). One implication is that the most stressful events are those over which the teacher has least control.

In England, Dunham (1976, 1977) has drawn attention to the stress induced by disruptive behaviour. He pointed out that many teachers 'are experiencing considerable frustration which they cannot express as aggressive behaviour, because the use by teachers of any sanctions against pupils is often tightly controlled'. This is a curious argument. Dunham seems to be implying that freedom to punish will result in reduction of stress. Yet informal observation suggests that the teachers who punish children most frequently, or most severely, may be an exceptionally highly stressed group. Dunham argues that because their frustration cannot be expressed directly, it is often expressed indirectly, in the form of psychosomatic symptoms such as headaches, body rashes or even depressive illness. Another common set of responses is feelings of inadequacy, loss of confidence or, in severe cases, panic. These, too, can be associated with psychosomatic symptoms. Like Simpson (1962), Dunham argued that absence due to illness was often a symptom of stress.

Dunham did not, however, seem to assume a direct causal link between disruptive behaviour and teacher stress. Earlier, we noted Borland's (1962) suggestion that disruptive behaviour might sometimes be the effect of teacher stress. Dunham accepted that disruptive behaviour increased teacher stress, but implied that both pupil disruptions and teacher stress were caused – or at least exacerbated – by other factors, both outside and within the school. The most important external factor was secondary reorganisation, with its consequent social and emotional upheaval for pupils and teachers alike.

The internal factors, in Dunham's view, were largely the result of this. He gave interesting examples of teachers who found themselves in two forms of role conflict. He termed the first 'intra-role conflict'. It is caused by conflicting demands from colleagues, for example when a head of department is under pressure from the head to retain mixed-ability teaching, and from her colleagues to return to banding by ability. 'Inter-role conflict', on the other hand, is particularly prevalent at the 'middle management' level of year tutor or head of house. If the teacher cannot reconcile the conflicting roles of teacher and counsellor, she may eventually doubt her ability to perform either one adequately.

Poor communications within the school have been seen as a source of stress by writers as diverse as Hargreaves (1978) and Dunham (1976). Indeed, it can be argued that poor communication between teachers, or between teachers and outside bodies, for example parents or the LEA administration, is at the root of most teacher stress. Poor communication is characterised either by *lack* of communication, which Hargreaves illustrates, or by destructive communication. In either case it helps to ensure that a potentially stressful incident escalates to a point at which it actually becomes stressful.

Intra-role conflict provides a good example. Changing to mixed-ability teaching from a traditional ability banding system is potentially stressful. How stressful it is in fact, will depend initially on the quality of communication between the head, the head of department and the subject teachers in the department. We say 'initially' because flexible, accessible channels of communication, in which everyone can express her hopes, frustrations or doubts without fear of criticism or ridicule are *necessary* for the prevention of stress, but not *sufficient*. Open communication can identify the problems which teachers anticipate, or are already experiencing. This is of limited value, though, unless it is used, in Kyriacou and Sutcliffe's (1978) terms, to develop more successful coping mechanisms. In other words, in the best remedial teaching tradition, the problem has to be identified in order to be tackled.

The same principles apply to the potential stress inherent in disruptive behaviour. The advice which inexperienced teachers receive on classroom discipline too often ranges between the banal: 'crack down hard to start with and then let up', to the disheartening: 'the first five years are the worst'. Interviews with teachers in ten Sheffield secondary schools left us in no doubt about the professional isolation of teachers in some schools when dealing with disruptive behaviour. Fortunately, this isolation, with its consequent stress, is not inevitable.

Teachers' experiences of disruptive behaviour

The incidents

We explained in Chapter 6 that we interviewed a random sample of teachers in each of the ten schools selected for intensive study. As well as asking the teachers about their experiences of special groups, we asked each teacher to 'describe the last incident in which a pupil or group of pupils presented you with any real problem'. Clearly, this called for a subjective judgement. When asked for clarification, the interviewer explained that we had in mind the last incident that had caused them genuine concern or stress, extending beyond the day-to-day problems that were an inevitable part and parcel of teaching. Subsequently, we asked whether they had sought support from colleagues and whether this support had helped them in dealing with the incident. If they had not sought support from colleagues we asked how they could obtain support, and the circumstances in which they would request it.

Analysis of the results showed that schools varied strikingly both in the severity of the incidents reported by teachers and in their recency. At school G, 33 per cent of teachers could not think of any incident which had cause them real concern in the current school year (most of the interviews took place in the spring term). At school J this applied to half the teachers interviewed. Both these schools belong to our group of three schools with exceptionally low exclusion rates. One teacher at school J remarked contentedly that 'this school's dead easy from a discipline point of view'. This was not because of low academic expectations. School J's pupils reported spending more time on homework than pupils at any of the other schools. School J was unique in our sample in being voluntary aided. Yet as the head-teacher remarked: 'the Catholic system has its share of problem families' – a claim which received indirect support from the number of pupils receiving free school meals.

In contrast, over 85 per cent of teachers at two other schools, A and C, could think of incidents which had caused them real concern in the current term. Frequently, the incident was within the previous fortnight. It was rare at these schools for a teacher to pause before answering the question. When they did pause, it was frequently to work out which of several recent incidents was the *most* recent.

The nature of the incidents, too, varied strikingly from school to school. Typical accounts from school I were:

'A fourth year boy; he just tended to wander around the lab, doing little work, if any. It wasn't a discipline situation, but he would make adverse comments.'

'A boy in the fifth year – wasn't making any effort and obviously didn't intend to. He'd "given up" as exams approached, not attending and so on.'

Similar incidents were reported by teachers in all schools. The striking point was that they seemed to be the norm at some schools and caused relatively little stress. At other schools the incidents were either more serious, or were symptomatic of a prolonged struggle, indicating an advanced state of exhausted frustration, often with an accompanying sense of futility:

It was this morning – not a major problem – it's an on-going one. They all are – something you deal with week in, week out. He had a rubber band he'd been flicking the other kids with. And he'd been smoking on the way to school this morning. He'd been on report twice before. The first time he lost the report form, and the second one he hasn't brought back to me yet – he was ill last week. So I gave him a third.

Occasionally, the confrontation was more blatant:

Two individuals were constantly disruptive . . . I told them they would stay in after school if they didn't work. They told me they wouldn't – and at four o'clock they both walked out.

(They were suspended for this incident.)

Sources of support

We asked about sources of support in dealing with disruptive behaviour. In theory the ten schools differed only in points of detail. In practice the differences were fundamental. They seemed to result partly from the school's explicit system for investigating and dealing with discipline problems. More important, though, they reflected teachers' perceptions of the attitudes of their colleagues, and in particular of their senior colleagues.

Tension arose in three schools because the formal channels for dealing with problem pupils were seen by many teachers as unsatisfactory. In one school many teachers seemed genuinely uncertain what the formal channels were. In two other schools the formal channels required the teacher to go first to the head of department. Thus, if a problem occurred in a maths lesson it would be referred to the head of the maths department. In practice, though, help was usually sought from pastoral care staff, as it was felt they were in a better position to take action. Pastoral care staff seemed generally to feel obliged to respond to these requests for help. In consequence, they were overworked, spending a very high proportion of their time investigating the problems of, and presented by, individual pupils. Their colleagues felt that something was being done, yet they seldom seemed to feel that they were – or needed to be – actively involved in the investigation or subsequent action. As a result, the support they received was indirect: they were able to refer a problem to a colleague, but seldom received, or expected, help in dealing with it themselves.

This problem also occurred to a lesser extent in three other schools, but was compounded by a widespread feeling that asking for support was a sign of weakness. At each school teachers made comments on the theme: 'There's a feeling that it's your own fault if you need help.' A newly qualified teacher said resignedly of some disruptive pupils in his class: 'You can threaten to send them to the deputy head, but you never do. It means you can't deal with it yourself.'

It is worth noting here that the policy in all six schools mentioned so far involved referral upwards. Faced with disruptive behaviour, teachers were expected to refer to the head of department or to the year tutor, who in turn would refer to a deputy head, who in turn would refer to the head. Particularly serious incidents would naturally be reported directly to the head, bypassing the earlier stages. Yet it was clear that less serious, even trival incidents could also come to the notice of the school's senior management. In two schools the deputy head responsible for boys' or girls' welfare was the appropriate person to whom to refer disruptive pupils. In one school this was because the year tutor's responsibilities appeared to be largely administrative; they were certainly not seen as a source of help or advice with problem children. In the other, a clear – but as we have already argued artificial – distinction between discipline and pastoral care meant that 'pastoral' problems were referred to year tutors while 'discipline' problems should be referred to a deputy head. The result was unsatisfactory in both cases. It meant that support and advice were too remote from teachers at the 'chalk face'. They felt isolated, and in many cases their morale suffered.

The other process whereby relatively trivial incidents could escalate to the attention of the head or his deputy was more subtle. We noted it briefly in Chapter 3, when discussing our study of pupils who had been suspended from school. A pupil could be referred to a year tutor or head of department for some relatively trivial incident. This in itself involved escalating the problem from a matter between child and teacher to a confrontation between child and middle management. If the child failed to cooperate with middle management, for example, by not turning up for detention, he would almost automatically be referred upwards, until the head himself became involved. Eventually, exclusion became inevitable, but by this time the original incident was all but forgotten.

Examples of exclusion resulting from this sort of escalation from a relatively minor incident occurred in schools B, C and H, all of which had exceptionally high exclusion rates. One head made clear that he saw it as no problem. He felt that the school had a system which worked very well for the great majority of pupils. If a disruptive minority defied that system there was really no choice – nor was there any problem. Quite obviously the school could not be run for the benefit of a tiny minority. They must simply leave, until they were willing to accept the school's rules and regulations. The head invariably explained his position to parents following exclusion. The majority accepted it, so that their children could return. A minority did not, so that exclusion escalated into suspension.

Faced with such apparent logic, it is worth asking how other schools not only managed to exclude or suspend very few pupils, but also managed to retain an atmosphere of stability. Our interviews with teachers suggested that the answer was unwritten, and possibly not always explicit recognised by the head. We can only describe it as a policy of 'de-escalation'. Instead of referring problems upwards, they were referred sideways, or even downwards. This happened in all three schools which excluded exceptionally few pupils, and also at school I, whose head was opposed to the idea of a special group.

Two processes seemed to be operating. In schools I and J, the form tutor was firmly enough established to be the obvious first source of advice. She was supposed to know not only all pupils in her tutor group, but also their parents. In school J the form tutor was responsible for checking that homework was completed. This was seen as a way of monitoring each pupil's progress. Failure to complete homework could be investigated to see whether the problem was confined to one particular subject, or formed part of a wider pattern associated with tensions either at home or at school. Thus, it was logical that the form tutor should be the first person to consult when a pupil presented a problem in the classroom. No one articulated the questions in as many words, but the orientation seemed to be: 'Why has this happened? What can we do about it?' The unspoken emphasis at some other schools was: 'This has happened. It must be investigated and dealt with.'

The second process was one of consultation between staff. Here, too, the emphasis was on preventing a problem from escalating into a major confrontation. At schools D and G the group teachers were involved in helping colleagues and pupils. A teacher at school D mentioned some objectionable behaviour from a boy in her class who was also attending the group. She had previously been asked not to get involved in a confrontation with this pupil, but to report any disruptive behaviour direct to the teacher in charge of the group. There would then be further discussion between the boy and the group teacher, and between the group teacher and the subject teacher. Another teacher at the same school told us about a boy whom a senior teacher had decided to cane for punching a girl in the face. The boy at first refused to accept punishment; after seeing the group teacher he eventually agreed on the condition that the group teacher acted as witness. Perhaps not all group teachers would have felt happy with this role. On the other hand, the boy realised he had offended. A confrontation was not in his interests any more than it was in the interests of the senior teacher concerned.

The tendency to adopt a low profile in cases of disruptive behaviour was also evident in school G. A form tutor was worried about racial tensions developing over a girl with an Italian mother. A number of girls were calling her a 'Wop bitch' and other offensive names. The teacher was thinking of sending the culprits to the senior mistress, but discussed the matter with her first. The senior mistress, however, advised caution. The form tutor should try to deal with the problem in class time by talking to the pupils concerned. Allowing it to escalate beyond the classroom could make the problem worse. The important point here is not that the senior mistress counselled against passing the problem upwards, but rather that the form tutor was able to discuss it with a senior colleague, and received advice and support in dealing with it herself.

We are not, of course, saying that the heads and deputy heads of schools D, G, I and J were never involved with incidents of disruptive behaviour. They certainly were – but only rarely, and only over incidents which required their personal involvement. Frequently, the purpose of the head-teacher's personal involvement was largely to bring home to the offender, or to his parents, the seriousness of the position. In the course of our work several head-teachers made the point that they could sometimes intervene successfully when everyone else had failed – but only because they were so seldom called upon to do so. If exclusion is a regular occurrence, it ceases to have much meaning, either for parents or for pupils. If it is used sparingly, its effect is dramatic, both on the individuals concerned and on the rest of the school.

Multiple stress – on pupils and teachers
Referring to the origins of deviant behaviour in childhood and adolescence, Rutter (1978) noted that children exposed to multiple stresses were more likely to display unacceptable behaviour patterns than children exposed to isolated stresses, however severe. The same principle applies in determining the degree of stress teachers experience from disruptive behaviour. To illustrate this, we must return to four potential sources of stress within a school.

First, the disturbing pupil is not a figment of a teacher's and psychologist's imagination – any more than the school's contribution in creating deviant behaviour is a figment of a sociologist's imagination. Some children do present learning and behaviour difficulties which result directly from constitutional and/or family problems. The evidence from our study of suspended pupils and their families is quite clear on this point. The critical question is not whether these children exist – they do – but how the school responds.to them.

Second, there are some schools in which some pupils are labelled failures, as a result either of policy or of practice. The distinction between policy and practice is not just semantic. The main thrust of

Hargreaves' (1967) argument, for example, was that an anti-school subculture developed because of a streaming policy which 'wrote off' a substantial minority of pupils as examination prospects. This did not happen as a matter of policy in any of the schools we studied. Nevertheless, no fewer than five suspended pupils from school C claimed in their own defence that they had been told they would not be allowed to take exams. This was true. From the school's point of view their attendance and behaviour had been so bad that it was a waste of time and money to allow them to take exams. From their point of view, however, the school was merely legitimising their attitude, both confirming and justifying their status in an anti-authority, educationally unsuccessful subgroup. The result was to increase stress both for pupils and for teachers. It gave the pupils a reputation to live down to, but this reputation inevitably brought them into conflict with teachers, and ultimately often with their parents as well. Teachers, too, suffered, since neither incentives nor sanctions were effective. Achieving demonstrably poor results with some of their classes, some teachers were clearly losing their professional confidence and pride.

The third potential source of stress we identified was the policy which facilitated escalation of problems. Designed as a way of supporting teachers, this policy often had the effect of reducing their confidence. Passing a problem to someone else does not increase your self-respect. A related issue is that the higher up you pass it, the more criticised you will feel if you do not receive support. One teacher gave a vivid description of incidents which had persuaded her not to seek support from colleagues:

> Quite honestly, I tend not to refer kids [for disruptive behaviour] if I can help it. It involves me in more hassle than it's worth. There's no trust in the relationships involved [i.e between the speaker and her senior colleagues]. A number of kids have been in the special group or out of the school altogether for swearing at the deputy – but if it is one of us it happens to, nothing is done. When I informed the head of a boy being rude to the school nurse, nothing was done. When the head saw a similar incident several months later, the boy was excluded at once.

Naturally, we cannot comment on the accuracy of this teacher's belief that 'nothing was done'. What matters is that she believed nothing was done. She had found herself in a Catch-22. She believed she would not be considered experienced enough to deal with the incident herself. The fact of referral to a more senior member of staff reflected her inexperience. The reaction – or lack of reaction – from the senior member of staff emphasised her inexperience. Teachers at some schools seemed able to ask colleagues for information about individual disruptive pupils, in a cooperative search for appropriate action. At other schools they seemed to feel that disruptive pupils should be referred to a more senior teacher for investigation and/or punishment. At other schools still, there was a feeling that the disruptive pupil simply should not be referred at all. The differences were unwritten, but the effect on teachers' morale was far-reaching.

The fourth potential source of stress follows from this. It could be described as the quality of a school's pastoral care for its own teachers. The quality of pastoral care for *pupils* can be determined: (a) by the degree to which each pupil feels he can take an educational or personal problem to a member of staff; (b) by the ability of teachers to recognise that the child has an educational or personal problem. In other words, each pupil needs to feel – and to be – valued in his own right. The same applies to teachers.

The quality of a school's pastoral care for its own teachers seemed to be directly linked to the quality of communication between teachers. The tone was set by the head and the deputy heads, but their lead was reflected through the school. This did not mean that they always accepted requests for help. A deputy head at school J, where a teacher described discipline as 'dead easy', made it clear that colleagues might be told quite firmly to raise the problem with the child's form teacher. The important thing was that the lines of communication should be recognised and used.

Tension can only be resolved when the issues are discussed openly. It may not be possible to reach a consensus, but it should be possible to make the reasons for a decision clear, and to assist staff in implementing any decision which affects them. This, of course, applies to all potential sources of teacher stress, not just disruptive behaviour. Both inter-role and intra-role conflict are examples. Similarly, unsatisfactory teaching conditions are much less dispiriting if you know that senior colleagues recognise them as unsatisfactory and are trying to do something about them.

Conclusions

At the start of this chapter we noted Borland's (1962) observation that disruptive behaviour can be either the cause or the effect of teacher stress. It might be more accurate to say that disruptive behaviour is sometimes an effect of teacher stress, but always causes more stress when it occurs. Our interviews with teachers suggests that in some schools they find themselves in a vicious circle of increasing stress.

Because of stresses within the school, such as poor communication networks or non-supportive relationships between staff, teachers start to doubt their achievements, to feel frustration at their conditions of service and to experience role conflict. This is really just another way of saying that their morale suffers. Pupils, as every teacher knows, are quick to sense a teacher's mood. They are also skilled in the art of 'divide and rule'. They recognise divisions within the staff, and exploit them. Teachers themselves recognise this. Many teachers made remarks like: 'They know they can't get away with it in my class,' or 'They know what happens if they step out of line.'

Low morale affects all aspects of teaching. One highly stressed teacher told us about a boy who had written pages of obscene graffiti in his exercise book. In one sense the boy had been justified, the teacher remarked resignedly. She hadn't been able to summon the energy to correct the work in his exercise book for over a fortnight.

We can see how the vicious circle establishes itself. Teachers' stress affects the pupils' sense of security and reduces their chances of achieving success from a well-planned lesson which is part of a well-designed curriculum. Pupils react to frustration in very much the same way that teachers themselves react – by becoming resentful and eventually losing their latent interest in their work. The resulting disruptive behaviour exploits the personal weaknesses in the teacher and the organisational or relationship weaknesses in the school's staff structure which contributed to the problem in the first place. Because these weaknesses still exist, disruptive behaviour causes increased stress for the teacher, which in turn is again communicated to the pupils.

This sorry scenario did not occur in all schools – nor even the majority. It did not affect all teachers in any school. However, it certainly did affect a substantial number of teachers in a minority of schools. It produced 'that distinctive, progressive *exhaustion*' against which Hargreaves (1978) reacted so strongly. We imply no disrespect or lack of consideration towards those teachers who were struggling under considerable stress to say that our results are nevertheless encouraging.

All schools occasionally face disruptive behaviour from pupils. Our evidence, reported in this chapter and in Chapters 5 and 6, suggests that the prevalence of disruptive behaviour is not predetermined by the pupils' social backgrounds. Policies, attitudes and practices within the school exert a substantial influence. As Reynolds et al. (1976) and Chapman (1979) claim: 'Schools do make a difference.' Equally encouraging, though not unexpected, was the evidence from teachers that the potential stress engendered by disruptive behaviour can be substantially reduced by the school's support networks, and by the overall quality of communication between teachers. Without doubt, disruptive behaviour from pupils is a potential source of stress. How stressful it actually becomes, depends largely on the nature and quality of relationships between the school's teachers.

Chapter 8

Implications for schools and for local education authority policy

Introduction

Teachers have little control over their pupils' background. They do have some control over the school's social climate. Family or 'intra-psychic' explanations have proved singularly unhelpful in understanding disruptive behaviour at school. We can look for, and in Chapter 3 we found, a wide range of problems in the pupils and in their families. Unfortunately, it is one thing to identify these problems, but another thing to solve them. Individual or family treatments such as counselling, psychotherapy or family case-work are less successful with socially deviant children or adolescents than with other groups.

The reasons are complex, but they all come back to one point. This is that the social, and in a school's case, the educational environment exerts a critical influence over the behaviour of the people who live or work in it. We are not saying that disadvantaged homes and delinquent neighbourhoods have *no* effect on pupils' behaviour at school. That would be absurd. We *are* saying that our own research confirms the evidence of other research teams in emphasising the school's own influence over its pupils' behaviour. A 'good' middle-class catchment area is no guarantee against disruptive behaviour. Nor does a depressed, inner-city catchment area containing a multitude of social problems guarantee a high level of disruptive behaviour. Some of the schools we observed had a high proportion of socially disadvantaged pupils. There was no sign of anarchy. They found little or no need to exclude or to suspend pupils. There seemed to be a cooperative relationship between pupils, between teachers and between teachers and pupils.

Local education authority policy

Short-term pressures
Exclusion or suspension from school creates an administrative prob-

lem for the LEA. The pupil's needs must be investigated, and in the case of suspension a decision made on his future education. The subject is also politically sensitive. Though for quite different reasons, both left- and right-wing politicians are interested in disruptive behaviour.

The trouble with politically sensitive issues and untidy administrative problems is that they tempt teachers, psychologists, administrators and politicians to carry out a superficial analysis in the search for a necessarily simplistic solution. No pupil's disruptive behaviour has a single cause. Suspended pupils frequently live in highly stressful family circumstances. Moreover, constitutionally they appear to be an exceptionally vulnerable group of pupils. Yet disruptive behaviour is seldom caused by family or constitutional stresses. It is caused by the interaction between these stresses and educational or social factors at school.

Faced with pressure from their own colleagues, from individual disruptive pupils, from parents of a more cooperative majority and from LEA administrators, some head-teachers would be less than human if they did not jump at a chance to earn at least a temporary respite by removing the most troublesome elements from the mainstream. Local education authority administrators face exactly the same sort of pressures except that they come from head-teachers, from parents of suspended pupils and occasionally from local councillors.

The greater the pressure, the greater the temptation to accept a simplistic solution. Separate facilities for disruptive pupils are a case in point. It is worth distinguishing here between off-site units established by the LEA to serve several schools and a special group which serves only the school which established it. Off-site units were seen as a way of catering for severely disruptive pupils when all other alternatives had been exhausted. The LEA had an obligation to these pupils. From political, administrative and ethical viewpoints, it was intolerable to pretend that they did not exist. The solution combined administrative expedience with humanity. There were only two snags.

The first snag was that off-site units could only cater for a minority of excluded or suspended pupils. Sheffield set up one such unit, catering for up to twenty pupils, staffed by six exceptionally able and experienced teachers. We saw in Chapter 2 what an embarrassingly small proportion of the city's most severely disruptive pupils were admitted to this centre. The second snag was the variation on Parkinson's law, noted in Chapter 1, which states that the number of disruptive pupils thought to need special facilities will continually increase to exceed the available supply.

In making these comments, we are not passing any judgement on the effectiveness of off-site units for the pupils admitted to them. They may be highly successful. That is a matter for further research. Our aim is merely to point out that they cannot realistically hope to cater for more than a minority of pupils for whom all other alternatives have been exhausted. Equally important, the referral process is arbitrary, since secondary schools vary so widely in their use of exclusion and suspension.

In their survey of 'behavioural units' HMI (1978) expressed uncertainty about the number of pupils returning to the mainstream, but implied that return was unlikely for older pupils. Virtually all pupils admitted to the Sheffield centre were regarded as 'terminal'; they would remain in the centre until they reached school-leaving age. From the referring head-teacher's point of view, this was often satisfactory. It was also acceptable from an administrative viewpoint, provided pupils were only admitted towards the end of their school careers, and hence could not occupy a place for too long.

Even if they can never be stated openly, LEA policy-makers should be clear about their reasons for opening off-site units. The first reason is that head-teachers have apparently demonstrated the need for such units by suspending pupils. Even if a unit only caters for a small proportion of the pupils concerned – as was the case in Sheffield – its value lies in creating a climate of opinion that 'something is being done'. Moreover, pupils undeniably *do* exist who have to be removed from secondary schools for their own or their school's good. The LEA should make provision for these pupils. The dilemma lies in the fact tht some schools produce a much larger number of these pupils than others. Removing them to a 'terminal' centre may help the pupils. It may also help the referring schools. But it does nothing to deal with the underlying tensions in the referring schools which may have contributed to the problem in the first place.

In the short run, everyone is satisfied with off-site units which are terminal in the sense that pupils will remain there until they reach school-leaving age. Pupils can be given an opportunity for success after – in many cases – nine or ten years of educational failure. Head-teachers can turn their attention to other problems. In the long run such units are of dubious value. Because they are terminal, their influence on the referring schools is minimal or non-existent. This pattern is not universal. Some centres do succeed in returning their pupils to the mainstream. Their success is due to the cooperation of referring schools. Requiring the referring school to cooperate in a pupil's rehabilitation may not endear an off-site unit, or the administration which sets it up, to the heads of all referring secondary schools. Yet, unless there is a constructive dialogue, it is hard to see how off-site units can be more than a sop to the public conscience, dealing with a minority of the worst, or perhaps just the most embarrassing, problems.

Special groups
When LEAs encourage schools to set up their own special groups they seem at first sight to overcome the major objections to off-site units. Unfortunately, we saw in Chapters 5 and 6 that considerable difficulties can arise even here. From an LEA policy viewpoint, an important observation in the Sheffield groups was that they had little or no effect on the number of suspensions or long-term exclusions. Another important observation, in the light of continuing public debate about corporal punishment, was that special groups were not, on the whole, used instead of more traditional sanctions. They were used when these sanctions had been tried and had failed.

At the very least, our evidence suggests that LEA policy-makers would be unwise to pin their faith on special groups if their main objective is to reduce the educational and administrative problems that result from exclusion or suspension. The same applies if their main objective is to help teachers to implement a policy of phasing out corporal punishment. The reasons are really very straightforward. Disruptive behaviour which results either in corporal punishment or in exclusion, generally occurs in the school's mainstream. Treating it out of context is illogical. When the problems arise at least in part because of social or educational stresses within the mainstream, special groups are in danger of diverting attention from the real problem area, namely the conditions which create the climate in which disruptive behaviour can flourish.

Encouraging a range of approaches
We have already noted that the head of one Sheffield school with no special group, told us that he had approached the LEA for assistance in helping his staff contain disruptive pupils within the ordinary classroom. The response had been discouraging, partly perhaps because of the economic climate, but partly also because his proposal did not involve setting up a group. The complex causes of disruptive behaviour imply a need for LEAs to recognise and encourage a range of approaches. However attractive one particular approach may look in theory, it cannot be expected to meet the needs of all schools. A special group may be needed for disruptive pupils in one school, providing a temporary respite for inexperienced teachers who have not acquired the skills in coping with these pupils. At another school a classroom-based intervention programme may seem more appropriate.

Sheffield has encouraged special groups with a wide range of objectives, with an equally wide range of methods. This indicates a healthy, far-sighted willingness to experiment both from the LEA and from individual schools. One hopes that this flexible approach will not be confined to special groups. Local education authority policy should actively promote a wide range of approaches, including those which explore the possibility of tackling the problem at source.

Delivery of support services
The implications for the delivery of support services can be stated briefly. First, the service should be provided in schools. Second, the underlying aim should be to cooperate with teachers in finding ways to handle the situation in school, and to prevent similar situations occurring in the future. This does not imply that individual counselling is unnecessary, nor that clinic-based treatment is always inappropriate. Case histories of slow learning and disruptive children show that both can be desirable (Galloway 1976c, 1981b).

Teachers and administrators will continue to need advice from, for example, educational psychologists on the educational needs of children who present exceptional problems. The emphasis in the support services is nevertheless changing. The central questions now are seldom: 'What is wrong with this child?' 'Why has he failed to adjust to the school?' Instead the questions are likely to be: 'Why has this problem occurred?' 'How can it be overcome, and similar problems prevented in future?' Treatment of the individual forms only one part of a comprehensive programme in which the system is expected to adapt to the needs of disruptive pupils, as well as the other way round.

Some effects of exclusion, suspension and special groups

Possibilities
The head-teacher's right to exclude pupils temporarily or to suspend them indefinitely is not in dispute. Nor should it be. The head-teacher's first obligation is to the majority of pupils and to his staff. One cannot legislate against crises, nor against chronic intransigence which pervades the whole school community. Hence, an essential effect of exclusion and suspension is to relieve pressure, both on teachers and on pupils in the main body of the school.

Ideally, the possibility of suspension should be sufficient to ensure its infrequent use. We saw in Chapter 2 that six of the 37 secondary schools studied neither suspended any pupils, nor excluded any for as long as three weeks, in the four years from 1975–79. Yet it is doubtful whether the heads of these schools would have been willing to forgo the right to suspend in an emergency. Similarly, the effect of a temporary exclusion varied widely from school to school. At some it was regarded almost as routine by pupils and teachers alike. At others, rarity ensured that it was treated as a major crisis. The latter approach seemed more effective in establishing a basis for future cooperation.

The head-teacher's right to remove a pupil from ordinary classes is no more in doubt than his right to exclude or suspend. Teachers are legally in *loco parentis*. If he feels that a pupil must be removed from an ordinary class for his own or his peers' good, the head has the right, and arguably an obligation, to do so. Special groups may be seen as providing a framework within which this can happen.

They would be difficult to justify, though, if their objectives were confined to containment. In principle they can offer a sanctuary for selected pupils who have been unable to cope with the demands of the school's ordinary classes. They can give pupils an experience of success, perhaps after many years of social and educational failure.

Placing a pupil in a special group may enable two processes to start. The first involves preparing the pupil for return to ordinary lessons. Thus, the retarded child may need to be taught to read. Similarly, the truculent teenager may need to be taught how to avoid antagonising his teachers. These are the remedial functions of the group. The second process is more difficult, and involves preparing *teachers* for the pupil's return. In saying this we are acknowledging the influence of teachers over their pupils' behaviour, not blaming them for disruptive behaviour. Gregory (1980) describes a pupil who illustrates our argument. The description is worth quoting in full:

> The referral of a 13-year-old boy from secondary school for behaviour problems . . . revealed that not all staff thought he warranted referral. When he was a problem, so were many others in the class, and the worst lesson was when they were in the library unsupervised. This part of the class was remedial. This mixed ability class was divided at this time to allow the brighter pupils to do modern languages whilst the remedial pupils went to the library where there were no books of an appropriate reading age. Here we have a time-table problem overcome by a 'library period'. Staff also admitted that mixed ability teaching was difficult, resulting in 'teaching to the middle' so that many remedial pupils were set work they could not do. The point is, again organisational problems of time-tabling, mixed ability teaching and inadequate management techniques of individual teachers were manifest in a single referral.

Gregory was talking about referral to an educational psychologist, but his analysis is equally valid for referral to special groups. Placing such a pupil in a special group could possibly have a moderate short-term benefit by removing one immediately obvious source of stress. Long-term benefit is also possible, though, if the special group provides a 'breathing space' in which teachers carry out the sort of assessment which Gregory describes. To do so, requires a high level of personal and professional maturity. It is much easier and less threatening to investigate, and inevitably to find, stresses in the child's home background.

Providing a 'breathing space' within which to carry out a careful assessment of contributory factors within the school is perhaps the most constructive use of special groups, and even of exclusion. The assessment is only a starting-point. Many of the solutions will necessarily be long-term ones. Returning to Gregory's example, resolution of timetabling problems will probably have to await the start of the next school year. Nor will problems arising from mixed-ability teaching have any immediate solution. In-service education, provision of adequate secretarial support in preparing materials, and establishing a staff-support network may all be needed.

Yet short-term palliative action is also possible, provided the problem is clearly enough recognised. Ensuring that pupils are set appropriate work, within their capability, in their unsupervised library period is one possibility. Another, which might send shudders of horror throughout the English department, is to provide comics for them to look at in the library, since no books have an appropriate reading age. If the head of the English department objects to children looking at comics in school time, he can be invited to find a better solution.

We are not, of course, suggesting that palliative action of this sort is any alternative to tackling the underlying problems, only that short-term action is a great deal better than nothing. Special groups which temporarily reduce pressure, so that teachers assess the problem and make the necessary adjustments, are potentially of enormous benefit to all concerned.

Pitfalls

The paradox of special groups and of exclusion or suspension is that as well as reflecting tensions within the school, they can also conceal these tensions. We have already seen how organisational problems which are not of a pupil's own making, may contribute to his disruptive behaviour. Returning once again to Gregory's (1980) example, problems in timetabling and mixed ability teaching were reflected in the behaviour of a thirteen-year-old boy. Referring the child to a psychologist, or excluding him or placing him in a special group is to individualise the problem. This may be both necessary and desirable, but only if the objective is to facilitate a careful assessment of the school's contribution in creating and solving the matter. The danger is that individualising the problem focuses attention on the pupil, and thereby diverts attention from what teachers can do to tackle it. This is the sense in which exclusion and special groups can conceal the tensions which create the need for them in the first place. In a nutshell, they can be self-perpetuating.

Superficially the problem is that both exclusion and special groups are responses to the behaviour of individual pupils. In discussion with parents they must almost inevitably be justified at this level. Almost inevitably, but not quite. Both parents and LEA administrators are generally willing to accept a head-teacher's decision to exclude, or to place a pupil in a special group, if this is seen as part of the school's preparation for his return to ordinary lessons. This was how one or two of the Sheffield schools enlisted parental support for their child's admission to a special group. They seldom, if ever, had any trouble. There is a temptation, though, to place a different emphasis on the matter. Parental support can be sought in helping the *child* adjust to the needs of the *school*. This was how the majority of Sheffield schools enlisted parental support. They, too, seldom had any trouble.

As we have argued, the pupil *does* sometimes need help, both educationally and socially. It is less than honest, though, to pretend that this is all that is needed. Both exclusion or suspension and special groups can be fatally easy ways of removing the evidence of underlying tensions. Removing the evidence will not make these underlying tensions go away. It can simply reduce the motivation to deal with them.

A good example is provided by the curriculum problems in the special groups we studied. In theory, subject teachers in all seven schools would provide work for the pupils to complete while attending the group. In practice we saw evidence of this actually happening in only one school. In at least four of the schools there was evidence that subject teachers had little inclination to play an active part in the pupil's rehabilitation. Yet the problem went deeper than this. When we looked at the work set by group teachers, it quickly became clear that many of the pupils were quite seriously backward educationally. Discussions both with group teachers and with subject teachers confirmed that many of the pupils had been failing academically before admission to a group. By implication, the curriculum and teaching methods in the pupils' original classes stood in need of review. The seven special groups in our sample had different underlying philosophies and used different methods. We were not convinced, however, that any of them facilitated this sort of review. Rather they seemed in many cases to obscure the need for it.

The value of exceptional children in helping teachers to understand their school's social and educational ecology is not always recognised. The very bright child challenges the teacher's ability to find interesting and stimulating material. The very dull child and the child with specific learning difficulties also challenge their teacher, though in a different way. In the field of behaviour, both disruptive and, hopefully, withdrawn children demand their teacher's attention.

These 'exceptional' children identify weaknesses in the teacher's curriculum and/or in her management techniques. The cooperative majority, presenting neither learning nor behavioural difficulties, will accept almost any diet they are offered, provided it offers them some hope of success in a teacher-directed activity. The willingness of pupils in all ages to spend hours wading through endless pages of 'sums' is a good example. Those pupils who defy the system, either by their disruptive behaviour, or by their failure to learn, raise questions about the system itself. Developing the 'sums' example, if retarded pupils benefit from a more varied, intrinsically stimulating approach to maths, it is reasonable to suppose that the majority may also benefit. In the same way, if a disruptive pupil benefits from his teacher's selective attention when he does something *right*, the other pupils may also benefit from more explicit and conscious recognition of their achievements.

The danger that special groups may enable teachers to overlook the issues which made them necessary in the first place is most acute when they become a long-term alternative to ordinary classes. We saw in Chapter 5 that the average period as a full-time member of the group varied from three to nineteen weeks. The longer a pupil remains out of ordinary classes, the less obligation his original teachers may feel to involve themselves actively in preparing for his return. A related problem is that special groups can easily turn into mini special schools, with all the disadvantages of special schools but few of the advantages.

Pastoral care: a comprehensive philosophy

Overcoming the false divide

We have argued that the need both for exclusion or suspension and for special groups can arise from tensions in the school's social and educational climate. Moreover, these tensions are not created by the pupils concerned. One implication is that disruptive behaviour must be seen in the context of the school's procedures for monitoring pupils' progress and for investigating and reacting to difficulties they encounter.

In Chapter 4 we argued that discipline and pastoral care should be seen as part of the same process, not as two separate processes. We also argued that concern for a pupil's educational progress at school was an integral aspect of his pastoral care. Distinguishing between discipline, pastoral care and academic progress makes neither educational or psychological sense. We are not, of course, denying that in practice decisions should sometimes be taken simply on disciplinary grounds. Temporary exclusion following an exceptionally serious incident is one example. With less serious incidents it is not always appropriate to investigate the circumstances before taking action. Immediacy can be a critical consideration.

Our point is that a pupil's behaviour at school, like his scholastic progress, constitutes an integral part of his educational welfare. Teachers are not social workers, and rapidly lose credibility when they try to behave like social workers. The central concern of pastoral care is for the pupil's welfare at school, not for his life out of school. Knowledge about family problems is often important, but only as an aid to meeting the child's educational needs at school. By definition, disruptive behaviour is behaviour which disturbs the school. Often, an immediate response is required for the school's benefit. A more considered response, though, will take the pupil's individual circumstances into account, both for the pupil's benefit and ultimately for that of the school.

In this model, pastoral care requires a wide-ranging knowledge of each pupil's adjustment and progress at school. It is not enough to know that Peter Smith has disturbed Mr Jones' chemistry lesson. The *fact* that he disturbed the lesson may justify a detention, as much for Mr Jones' benefit as Peter's. Whether the matter should be allowed to rest there depends on other considerations. We need to know, for example, whether Mr Jones has problems with a lot of pupils, whether Peter's disruptive behaviour in chemistry is confined to that lesson or is part of a wider pattern, and so on.

In discussing this concept of pastoral care with teachers we were sometimes accused of inconsistency. We were proposing, they claimed, a highly individualised notion of pastoral care. Yet in the previous breath we had been attacking individualised theories about the causation of disruptive behaviour, claiming that the school's social and educational climate was the crucial variable. We denied any inconsistency! A school's educational and social climate is determined to a large extent by the progress and achievements of each individual pupil, and by the extent to which each individual pupil feels that his difficulties are recognised and his achievements valued. This is quite different from saying that problems at school are caused by personal or family factors over which the school has no control.

Unfortunately, procedures at some schools do little to facilitate a comprehensive understanding of each pupil. Three principal issues emerged from our study of ten schools. All have been discussed in earlier chapters, and need only be summarised here.

(a) The 'official channels' in some schools required teachers to advise their head of department over a disciplinary problem and the year tutor or head of year over a pastoral one. Because the distinction was conceptually invalid, it proved difficult to operate in practice.

(b) The 'official channels' often seemed to carry a built-in escalation clause. If you were going to seek help or support from a colleague, you sought it from a senior colleague, at least at middle management level. In turn this led to a related problem. First, it created a climate in which teachers felt they could refer a pupil *to* a colleague, with the implication – which the colleague often resented – that she would investigate and deal with the problem. This seemed to contrast with the climate in other schools which encouraged teachers to discuss problem pupils *with* colleagues, with the implication that the teacher might be able to deal with it herself. A logical result was that relatively minor issues could escalate from a dispute between a subject teacher and pupil to a confrontation between the head and the pupil, culminating in exclusion or suspension.

(c) In some schools the form tutor's role as the primary unit of pastoral care appeared to be undervalued by the policy of referring problems upwards. More seriously, organisational decisions sometimes made it impossible for form tutors to play any important part in their pupil's pastoral care. This could happen in at least three ways. First, a policy whereby form tutors changed every year or every alternate year, reduced the sense of continuity which is desirable in pastoral care. Second, the time available to form tutors sometimes prevented them from doing much more than complete the attendance register. Third, all 'important' discussions about a pupil were the virtually exclusive preserve of senior or middle management. A conscientious form tutor could take an active interest in the pupils in his tutor group. School policy tolerated this, but sometimes did little or nothing to encourage it.

The form tutor's importance may be gauged from the facts:

(a) that each pupil might be taught by as many as twelve teachers in the course of the week, none of whom would see him more than three or four times; (b) that the year tutor might have up to 400 pupils in her year. In contrast form tutors would see their pupils twice daily for registration purposes, and in some schools for one or two form periods a week as well. Whether a large school is an impersonal school depends largely on the scope and the pastoral skills of form tutors.

This does not negate the role of the year tutor or head of house. It implies that they should see themselves as leaders, or coordinators, of a team of form tutors. Two head-teachers described their year tutors or heads of houses as mini heads of school. How well this worked in practice depended partly on the people concerned and partly on organisational or policy factors over which they had no direct control. In Chapter 6 we described two schools in which it seemed to work very well indeed, but this was not the picture everywhere.

Pastoral care – for teachers as well as pupils

A head-teacher might quite reasonably state his primary concern as the pastoral care of his pupils. Just as reasonably, he might define his primary concern as the pastoral care of his teachers. At the risk of sounding banal, unhappy teachers cannot create a happy school. Teachers who themselves feel undervalued are unlikely to value individuality in their pupils. Teachers who no longer set themselves high standards cannot recognise, let alone develop, the full potential in their pupils. To think about the pastoral care of pupils without considering the pastoral care of teachers is illogical. Successful pastoral care for pupils is a pipe-dream if their teachers have lost their professional confidence or their personal security.

We argued in Chapter 7 that some of the teachers we interviewed were experiencing severe stress. The main purpose of our interviews was to inquire about teachers' recent experiences of disruptive behaviour, and their views on discipline and pastoral care. Not surprisingly, disruptive behaviour was frequently associated with stress. Of more interest, disruptive behaviour seemed to generate most severe stress when the networks for support and consultation between teachers were inflexible or not clearly understood. Teachers, like pupils, need to feel there is someone with whom they can discuss a problem before it becomes too serious. The requirement is not that someone should solve the problem – that would be as unreasonable for teachers with discipline problems as it would be for pupils from chronically disadvantaged families – but to air the problem and explore possible ways of relieving it.

Conclusions

We hope that teachers will find the results reported in this book encouraging. Teachers *do* make a difference! Yet the results are also challenging, and hence threatening in both a personal and a professional sense. In summarising the implications of our own work and of some of the other work we have described, four issues seem of critical importance.

1. The problem of disruptive behaviour is most readily solved by prevention. Punishment may sometimes be necessary, but it has two inherent limitations. First, punishment, by definition, involves acting after the event. Related to this, and more serious, punishment can be effective in teaching pupils what *not* to do, but cannot teach them how they *should* behave. Moreover, punishments can be self-defeating, either because they are used too frequently and hence lose their symbolic importance for pupils and teachers alike, or because they unify pupils in opposition to the school's values. We saw evidence that both exclusion and corporal punishment had this effect in a minority of schools.

2. On our evidence, special groups cannot reasonably be seen as a solution to the problems which disruptive pupils cause in school. Nor will they solve the LEA's problems by preventing the perceived need for exclusion or suspension. Special groups can be a valued source of support, both for pupils and for teachers. To be effective they require the active support of the school's senior management, and also a cooperative, informal relationship between the teacher in charge and his colleagues. When teachers have greeted with relief a pupil's removal to a special group, the difficulty in persuading them to cooperate actively in his return should not be underestimated.

3. Neither teachers with special responsibility for pastoral care, nor school counsellors, are likely to make much impact on the level of disruptive behaviour if they confine their activities to counselling individual pupils on personal or behavioural matters. Effective pastoral care embraces all aspects of a pupil's welfare at school – his educational progress, his behaviour and an understanding of family or other out-of-school factors which may affect his progress and adjustment at school. *All* pupils require effective pastoral care. This clearly cannot be provided by year tutors or heads of houses. Unfortunately the organisation of form tutor groups in some schools makes it difficult or impossible for form tutors to provide effective pastoral care.

4. When a number of older pupils develop an anti-authority identity, this presents a problem *for* the school. It should also be recognised as a problem *of* the school. Both in our study of pupils suspended

from school and in our study of special groups, we interviewed pupils who regarded themselves as members of educationally unsuccessful, anti-authority subgroups. In all cases, this seemed to arise from a perception that the school had rejected them, was making unreasonable or petty demands (for example over uniform), or was offering a curriculum irrelevant to their needs. An obvious, and uncontroversial implication is that all pupils should feel that the school values their achievements. The least able pupil needs high-quality teaching at least as much as the brightest. When less care and importance is attached to classes of less able pupils, the pupils themselves recognise this even before their teachers.

Tackling problem behaviour through the school's policy, organisation and ethos is not wishful thinking. The Sheffield studies showed that some schools, including some which served difficult catchment areas, apparently felt little or no need to exclude or suspend pupils. We further argued that some schools were able to prevent disruptive incidents from escalating into serious confrontations. There was no evidence to suggest that these schools expected, or received, less from their pupils in academic terms. While our work gives no cause for complacency, it does suggest that teachers have a great deal more influence than is often supposed over the behaviour of their potentially disturbing pupils.

Rutter (1978) points out that: 'Single chronic stresses are surprisingly unimportant if the stresses really are isolated.' To give an example, illustrating this point, a child may be able to cope with severe family friction if he feels that at school his achievements are recognised by teachers who are sympathetically aware of the stress at home. If the same child does not experience success at school, for any of the reasons we have discussed throughout this book, he may well present the school – and himself – with problems. If this happens, it will be understandable if his teachers seek an explanation in his background, but this will tell them no more than half the story, and may cause them to feel unnecessarily pessimistic about their own ability to relieve the situation.

References

Abbreviations

Behav. Psychother.	*Behavioural Psychotherapy*
Behav. Res. Ther.	*Behaviour Research and Therapy*
Brit. J. Criminol.	*British Journal of Criminology*
Brit. J. Educ. Psychol.	*British Journal of Educational Psychology*
Brit. J. Psychiat.	*British Journal of Psychiatry*
Bull. Brit. Assoc. Behav. Psychother.	*Bulletin of the British Association for Behavioural Psychotherapy*
Bull. Brit. Psychol. Soc.	*Bulletin of the British Psychological Society*
Educ. Res.	*Educational Reasearch*
Educ. Rev.	*Educational Review*
J. Appl. Behav. Anal.	*Journal of Applied Behavioural Analysis*
J. Child Psychol. Psychiat.	*Journal of Child Psychology and Psychiatry*

Anderson, E. (1973) *The Disabled Schoolchild: a study of integration in primary schools*. London: Methuen.

Anon (1980) 'Disruptive' children greatest source of stress, *American Teacher* 64 (iv) 17.

Archer, W. N. (1973) *A study of the effects of a remedial teaching programme for maladjusted children in normal primary schools*. Unpublished Dissertation for University of London Diploma in Education with special reference to children up to the age of thirteen years. London: Maria Grey College.

Baldwin, J. (1972) Delinquent schools in Tower Hamlets I: a critique, *Brit. J. Criminol.* **12**, 399–401.

Bennett, N. (1976) *Teaching Styles and Pupil Progress*. London: Open Books.

Berg, I., Consterdine, M., Hullin, R. and McGuire, R. (1978) The effect of two randomly allocated court procedures on truancy, *Brit. J. Criminol.* **18**, 232–44.

Berger, M. (1979) Behaviour modification in education and professional practice: the dangers of a mindless technology, *Bull. Brit. Psychol. Soc.* **32**, 418–19.

Borland, N. R. (1962) Discipline and strain, *National Education (New Zealand)* **44**, 165–70.

Brown, G. W. Bhrolcháin, M. N. and Harris, J. (1975) Social class and psychiatric disturbance among women in an urban population, *Sociology* **9**, 225–54.

Burland, J. R. (1978) The evolution of a token economy in a residential school for maladjusted junior boys, *Behav. Psychother.* **6**, 97–104.

Callaghan, J. (1976) Speech by the Prime Minister, the Rt Hon. James Callaghan, MP, at a Foundation Stone-laying Ceremony at Ruskin College, Oxford, on Monday 18 October (press release)

Caspari, I. E. (1976) *Troublesome Children in Class*. London: Routledge and Kegan Paul.

Cattell, R. B. and Cattell, M. D. L. (1975) *Handbook for the High School Personality Questionnaire*. Champaign, Ill.: Institute for Personality and Ability Testing.

Chapman, B. L. M. (1979) Schools do make a difference, *British Educational Research Journal* **5**, 115–24.

Cichon, D. J. and Koff, R. H. (1980) Stress and teaching, *National Association of Secondary School Principals Bulletin* **66**, 91–104.

Cicourel, A. V. and Kitsuse, J. I. (1968) The social organisation of the high school and deviant adolescent careers. In: Rubington, E. and Weinberg, M. (eds) *Deviance: The Interactionist Perspective*. New York: Macmillan.

Clarke, R. V. G. and Cornish, D. B. (1978) The effectiveness of residential treatment for delinquents. In: Hersov, L., Berger, M. and Schaffer, D. (eds) *Aggression and Anti-social Behaviour in Childhood and Adolescence*. Oxford: Pergamon.

Clegg, A. and Megson, B. (1968) *Children in Distress*. Harmondsworth: Penguin.

Cline, T. (1980) More help for schools: a critical look at child guidance, *Therapeutic Education* **8** (i) 3–11.

Coard, B. (1971) *How the West Indian Child is Made Educationally Sub-normal in the British School System.* London: New Beacon Books.

Cobb, S. and Rose, R. M. (1973) Hypertension, peptic ulcer and diabetes in air traffic controllers, *The Journal of the American Medical Association* **224**, 489–92.

Coleman, J. S. et al. (1966) *Equality of Educational Opportunity.* Washington: US Government Printing Office.

Cooling, M. (1974) *Educational provisions for maladjusted children in boarding schools.* M. Ed. Thesis, Birmingham University.

Cornish, D. B. and Clarke, R. V. G. (1975) *Residential Treatment and its Effects on Delinquency.* London: HMSO.

Craft, M. (1965) A follow-up study of disturbed juvenile delinquents, *Brit. J. Criminol.* 5, 55–62.

Dain, P. (1977) Disruptive children and the Key Centre, *Remedial Education* **12** (iv), 163–7.

Davie, E. R., Butler, N. and Goldstein, H. (1972) *From Birth to Seven,* London: Longman.

Davies, J. A. V. and Maliphant, R. (1974) Refractory behaviour in school and avoidance learning, *J. Child Psychol. Psychiat.* 15, 23–31.

Delamont, S. (1976) *Interaction in the Classroom.* London: Methuen Contemporary Sociology of the School.

Department of Education and Science (1966) *The Health of the School Child 1964–65.* London: HMSO.

Department of Education and Science (1967) *Children and their Primary Schools* (The Plowden Report). London: HMSO.

Department of Education and Science (1968) *Psychologists in Education Services* (The Summerfield Report). London: HMSO.

Department of Education and Science (1973) *Staffing of Special schools and classes,* Circular 4/73, London: HMSO.

Department of Education and Science (1975) *The Discovery of Children Requiring Special Education and the Assessment of Their Needs,* Circular 2/75, London: DES.

Department of Education and Science (1976) *Statistics of Education 1976,* vol. 1, *Schools.* London: HMSO.

Department of Education and Science (1978) *Special Educational Needs* (The Warnock Report). London: HMSO.

Dunham, J. (1976) Stress situations and responses. In: National Association of Schoolmasters and Union of Women Teachers (eds) *Stress in Schools.* Hemel Hempstead: NAB/UWT.

Dunham, J. (1977) The effects of disruptive behaviour on teachers, *Educ. Rev.* **29**, 181–7.

Education Act (1921) 11 & 12 Geo. V, c. 51, London: HMSO.

Education Act (1944) 7 & 8 Geo. VI, c. 31, London: HMSO.

Eisenberg, L., Connors, K. and Sharpe, L. (1965) A controlled study of the differential application of out-patient psychiatric treatment for children, *Japanese Journal of Child Psychiatry* **6**, 125–32.

Farrington, D. (1972) Delinquency begins at home, *New Society* **21**, 14 September, 495–97.

Finlayson, D. J. (1973) Measuring school climate, *Trends in Education* **30** (April) 19–27.

Finlayson, D. S. and Loughran, J. L. (1976) Pupils' perceptions in high and low delinquency schools, *Educ. Res.* **18**, 138–44.

Fitzherbert, K. (1977a) Unwillingly to school, *New Society* **39**, 17 February, 332–4.

Fitzherbert, K. (1977b) *Child Care Services and the Teacher.* London: Maurice Temple Smith.

Fixsen, D. L., Phillips. E. L. and Wolf, M. (1973) Achievement place: experiments in self-government with pre-delinquents, *J. Appl. Behav. Anal.* **6**, 31–47.

Flanders, N. A. C. (1970) *Analysing Teaching Behavior.* Reading, Mass: Addison-Wesley.

Fogelman, K. (1976) *Britain's Sixteen Year Olds.* London: National Children's Bureau.

Galloway, D. M. (1975) A behavioural approach to treatment, *Therapeutic Education* **3**, No. 2, 23–31.

Galloway, D. M. (1976a) Size of school, socio-economic hardship, suspension rates and persistent unjustified absence from school, *Brit. J. Educ. Psychol.* **46**, 40–7.

Galloway, D. M. (1976b) Persistent unjustified absence from school, *Trends in Education* **4**, 22–7.

Galloway, D. M. (1976c) *Case Studies in Classroom Management.* London: Longman.

Galloway, D. M. (1977) Application of behavioural analysis and behaviour modification in school psychological service practice, *Bull. Brit. Assoc. Behav. Psychother.* **5**, 63–6.

Galloway, D. M. (1980a) *A study of persistent absence from school in Sheffield: prevalence and associated educational, psychological and social factors.* Unpublished Ph.D Thesis. CNAA: Sheffield City Polytechnic.

Galloway, D. M. (1980b) Problems in the assessment and management of persistent absence from school. In: Hersov, L. and Berg, I. (eds) *Out of school.* London: Wiley.

Galloway, D. M. (1981a) Institutional change or individual change? An overview. In: Gillham, B. (ed.) *Problem Behaviour in the Secondary School: A Systems Approach.* London: Croom Helm.

Galloway, D. M. (1981b) *Teaching and Counselling.* London: Longman.

Galloway, D. M. (1981c) Sheffield School and Home Project: summary and implications of completed research, *Journal of the Association of Educational Psychologists* (in press).

Galloway, D. M., Ball, C. and Seyd, R. (1978) Absence from school and behaviour problems at school, *Therapeutic Education* **6** (ii), 18–34.

Galloway, D. M. and Goodwin, C. (1979) *Educating Slow-learning and Maladjusted Children: Integration or Segregation?* London: Longman.

Galloway, D. M., Martin, R. and Wilcox, B. (1981a) Persistent absence from school and exclusion from school: the predictive power of school and community variables (in preparation).

Galloway, D. M., Ball, C. and Seyd, R. (1981b) The selection of parents and children for legal action in connection with unauthorised absence from school, *British Journal of Social Work* (in press).

Galloway, D. M., Ball, C. and Seyd, R. (1981c) Some implications for social workers of recent research on poor school attendance, *Social Work Today* **12** (xxxiii), 15–17.

Galway, J. (1979) What pupils think of special units, *Comprehensive Education* **39**, No. 375, 18–20.

Gath, D., Cooper, B. and Gattoni, F. E. G. (1972) Child guidance and delinquency in a London borough: preliminary communication, *Psychological Medicine* **2**, 185–91.

Gath, D., Cooper, B., Gattoni, F. and Rockett, D. (1977) *Child Guidance and Delinquency in a London Borough.* Oxford: Oxford University Press.

Gathorne-Hardy, J. (1977) *The Public School Phenomenon.* London: Hodder and Stoughton.

Gillham, B. (1978) The failure of psychometrics. In: Gillham, B. (ed.) *Reconstructing Educational Psychology.* London: Croom Helm.

Goffman, E. (1961) *Asylums.* New York: Anchor.

Golby, M. (1979) Special units: some educational issues, *Socialism and Education* **6** (ii), 6–9.

Gough, R. G. (1974) *The induction year – a sociological focus.* Unpublished M.Sc. (Econ.) Thesis. University of London: Institute of Education.

Graham, P. and Rutter, M. (1968a) The reliability and validity of the psychiatric study of the child: II. Interview with the parent, *Brit. J. Psychiat.* **114**, 581–92.

Graham, P. and Rutter, M. (1968b) Organic brain dysfunction and child psychiatric disorder, *British Medical Journal* 3, 695–700.

Graham, P. and Rutter, M. (1970) Selection of children with psychiatric disorder, in M. Rutter, J. Tizard and K. Whitmore (1970) (eds) *Education, Health and Behaviour*, London: Longman.

Gregory, R. P. (1980) Individual referrals: How naive are educational psychologists? *Bull. Brit. Psychol. Soc.* **33**, 381–4.

Griffin, D. (1978) *Slow learners: A break in the circle*. London: Woburn Press.

Grunsell, R. (1978) *Born to be Invisible: The Story of a School for Truants*. London: Macmillan Education.

Grunsell, R. (1979) Suspensions and the sin-bin boom, *Where* **153**, 307–09.

Haggerty, M. E. (1925) The incidence of undesirable behaviour in public-school children, *Journal of Educational Research* **12**, 102–22.

Hamblin, D. H. (1977) Caring and control: the treatment of absenteeism. In: Carroll, H. C. M. (ed.) *Absenteeism in South Wales: Studies of Pupils, their Homes and their Secondary Schools*. Swansea: Faculty of Education, University College of Swansea.

Hansard Parliamentary Debates (1975) 863, p. 105. London: HMSO.

Hare, R. D. (1970) *Psychopathy: Theory and Research*. New York: Wiley.

Hargreaves, D. H. (1967) *Social Relationships in a Secondary School*. London: Routledge and Kegan Paul.

Hargreaves, D. H. (1978) What teaching does to teachers, *New Society*, **43**, 9 March, 540–2.

Hargreaves, D. H. Hestor, S. K. and Mellor, F. J. (1975) *Deviance in Classrooms*. London: Routledge and Kegan Paul.

Harris, R. (1978) Relationship between EEG abnormality and aggressive and anti-social behaviour – a critical appraisal. In: Hersov, L. A., Berger, M. and Shaffer, D. (eds) *Aggression and Anti-social Behaviour in Childhood and Adolescence*. Oxford: Pergamon.

Harrop, L. A. (1980) Behaviour modification in schools: a time for caution, *Bull. Brit. Psychol. Soc.* **33**, 158–60.

Heal, K. H. (1978) Misbehaviour among school children: the role of the school in strategies for prevention, *Policy and Politics*, **6**, 321–32.

Hebb, D. O. (1972) *Textbook of Psychology* (3rd edn). Philadelphia: Saunders.

Her Majesty's Stationery Office (1972) *Statistics relating to Approved Schools, Remand Homes and Attendance Centres in England and Wales for the Year 1970*. London: HMSO.

Her Majesty's Inspectorate of Schools (1978) *Behavioural Units*. London: Department of Education and Science.

Hersov, L. (1960) Persistent non-attendance at school, *J. Child Psychol. Psychiat.* **1**, 130–6.

Hersov, L. (1977) School refusal. In: Rutter, M. and Hersov, L. (eds) *Child Psychiatry: Modern Approaches*. Oxford: Blackwell.

Holman, P. and Libretto, G. (1979) The On-Site Unit, *Comprehensive Education* **39**, No. 375, 10–12.

Hood-Williams, J. (1960) The results of psychotherapy with children: a revaluation, *Journal of Consulting Psychology* **24**, 84–8.

Inner London Education Authority (1965) *Survey into progress of maladjusted children*, London: ILEA.

Jones, N. (1971) The Brislington Project at Bristol, *Special Education* **60** (ii), 23–6.

Jones, N. (1973) Special adjustment units in comprehensive schools: I. Needs and resources. II. Structure and function, *Therapeutic Education* **1**, No. 2, 23–31.

Jones, N. (1974) Special adjustment units in comprehensive schools: III. Selection of children, *Therapeutic Education* **2**, No. 2, 21–6.

Kligman, D. and Goldberg, D. A. (1975) Temporal lobe epilepsy and aggression, *Journal of Nervous and Mental Disorders*, **160**, 324–41.

Kounin, J. S. (1970) *Discipline and Group Management in Classrooms*. New York: Holt, Rinehart and Winston.

Kyriacou, C. and Sutcliffe, J. (1977) Teacher stress: a review, *Educ. Rev.* **29**, 299–306.

Kyriacou, C. and Sutcliffe, J. (1978) A model of teacher stress, *Educational Studies*, **4**, 1–6.

Kyriacou, C. and Sutcliffe, J. (1979) Teacher stress and satisfaction, *Educ. Res.* **21**, 89–95.

Labon, D. (1973) Helping maladjusted children in primary schools, *Therapeutic Education* **1**, No. 2, 14–22.

Labon, D. (1974) Some effects of school-based therapy, *Association of Educational Psychologists Journal* **3** (vi) 28–34.

Lane, D. (1977) Aspects of the use of behaviour modification in secondary schools, *Bull. Brit. Assoc. Behav. Psychother.* **5**, 76–9.

Lane, D. A. and Millar, R. (1977) Dealing with behaviour problems in school: a new development, *Community Health* **8**, 155–8.

Lane, H. (1928) *Talks to Parents and Teachers*. London: Allen and Unwin.

Lawrence, J. (1978) *Exploring techniques for coping with disruptive behaviour in schools*. London: University of London: Goldsmiths' College.

Lawrence, J., Steed, D. and Young, P. (1977) *Disruptive behaviour in a Secondary School*. London: University of London: Goldsmiths' College.

Laycock, A. J. (1968) Vascular change under stress in delinquents and controls, *Brit. J. Criminol.* **8**, 64–9.

Lazarus, R. S. (1967) Cognitive and personality factors underlying threat and coping. In: Appley, M. H. and Trumbull, R. (eds) *Psychological Stress*. New York: Appleton.

Lemert, E. M. (1967) *Human Deviance: Social Problems and Social Control*. Englewood Cliffs: Prentice-Hall.

Levitt, E. E. (1957) Results of psychotherapy with children: an evaluation, *Journal of Consulting Psychology* **21**, 189–96.

Levitt, E. E. (1963) Psychotherapy with children: a further evaluation, *Behav. Res. Ther.* **1**, 45–51.

Lloyd-Smith, M. (1979) The meaning of special units, *Socialism and Education* **6** (ii), 10–11.

Local Government Training Board (1972) *Training of Educational Welfare Officers: Training Recommendation 19*. Luton: Local Government Training Board.

Lodge, B. (1977) Call to isolate the classroom thugs, *Times Educational Supplement*, 15 April.

Longworth-Dames, S. M. (1977) The relationship of personality and behaviour to school exclusion, *Educ. Rev.* **29**, 163–77.

Lowenstein, L. F. (1975) *Violent and Disruptive Behaviour in Schools*. Hemel Hempstead: National Association of Schoolmasters.

McFie, B. S. (1934) Behaviour and personality difficulties in school children, *Brit. J. Educ. Psychol.* **4**, 30–46.

McMichael, P. (1974) After-care, family relationships and reconviction in a Scottish approved school, *Brit. J. Criminol.* **14**, 236–47.

Meighan, R. (1978) A pupils' eye view of teaching performance, *Educ. Rev.* **30**, 125–37.

Milner, M. (1938) *The Human Problem in Schools*. London: Methuen.

Ministry of Education (1945) *The Handicapped Pupils and School Health Service Regulations* (S. R. and O. No. 1076). London: HMSO.

Mitchell, S. and Rosa, P. (1981) Boyhood behaviour problems as precursors of criminality: a fifteen year follow-up, *J. Child Psychol. Psychiat.* **22**, 19–33.

Newell, P. (ed.) (1979) *Corporal Punishment in Schools: Aboliton Handbook*. Croydon: Society of Teachers Opposed to Physical Punishment.

Newman, G. R. and Wilkins, L. T. (1974) Sources of deviance in the schooling process, *International Review of Education* **20**, 306–21.

New Zealand Educational Institute (1975) *Children's Behaviour: Its Modification by Teacher, Parent and Peer* (NZEI Yearbook of Education No. 4). Wellington: NZEI.

O'Leary, K. D. and O'Leary, S. C. (eds) (1979) *Classroom Manage-*

ment: *The Successful Use of Behaviour Modification* (2nd edn). New York: Pergamon.

Pallister, R. (1969) The determinants of elementary school attendance about 1850, *Durham and Newcastle Research Review* 5, 384–98.

Phillips, E. L. (1968) Achievement Place: token reinforcement procedures in a home-style rehabilitation setting for pre-delinquent boys, *J. Appl. Behav. Anal.* 1, 213–23.

Phillips, E. L., Phillips E. A., Fixsen, D. L. and Wolf, M. (1973) Behaviour shaping works with delinquents, *Psychology Today* June., 74–90.

Phillips, E. L., Wolf, M. M., Fixsen, D. L. and Bailey, J. S. (1976) Achievement Place Model: A community-based, family-style, behaviour modification-programme for pre-delinquent youth. In Ribes-Inesta, E. and Bandura, A. (eds) *Analysis of Delinquency and Aggression.* Hillsdale N.J: Erlbaum.

Phillipson, C. M. (1971) Juvenile delinquency and the school. In: Carson, W. G. and Wiles, P. (eds) *Crime and Delinquency in Britain: Sociological readings.* London: Martin Robertson.

Pick, M. (1974) School for truants, *The Guardian* 19 February.

Power, M. J., Alderson, M. R., Phillipson, C. M., Schoenberg, E. and Morris, J. M. (1967) Delinquent schools, *New Society,* 10, 19 October, 542–3.

Power, M. J., Benn, R. T. and Morris, J. M. (1972) Neighbourhood, school and juveniles before the courts, *Brit. J. Criminol.* 12, 111–32.

Pratt, J. (1978) Perceived stress among teachers: the effects of age and background of children taught, *Educ. Rev.* 30, 3–14.

Reynolds, D. (1976) When pupils and teachers refuse a truce: the secondary school and the creation of delinquency. In: Mungham, G. and Pearson, G. (eds) *Working Class Youth Culture.* London: Routledge and Kegan Paul.

Reynolds, D. Jones, D. and St. Leger, S. (1976) Schools do make a difference, *New Society* 37, 321.

Reynolds, D. and Murgatroyd, S. (1977) The sociology of schooling and the absent pupil: the school as a factor in the generation of truancy. In: Carroll, H. C. M. (ed.) *Absenteeism in South Wales: Studies of Pupils, their Homes and their Secondary Schools.* Swansea: University College of Swansea, Faculty of Education.

Robins, L. N. (1966) *Deviant Children Grown Up.* Baltimore: Williams and Wilkins.

Robins, L. N. (1972) Follow-up studies of behaviour disorder in children. In: Quay, H. C. and Werry, J. S. *Psychopathological Disorders of Childhood.* New York: Wiley.

Rogers, V. R. and Barron, J. (1976) Questioning the evidence, *Times Educational Supplement*, 30 April, 20–1.

Rotenberg, M. (1974) Self-labelling: a missing link in the 'Societal reaction' theory of deviance, *Sociological Review* 22, 335–54.

Rowan, P. (1976) Short-term sanctuary, *Times Educational Supplement*, 2 April, 21–4.

Rutter, M. (1965) Classification and categorisation in child psychiatry, *J. Child Psychol. Psychiat.* 6, 71–83.

Rutter, M. (1966) *Children of Sick Parents: An Environmental and Psychiatric Study*. Institute of Psychiatry, Maudsley Monographs No. 16. London: Oxford University Press.

Rutter, M. (1967) A children's behaviour questionnaire for completion by teachers: preliminary findings, *J. Child Psychol. Psychiat.* 8, 1–11.

Rutter, M. (1977) Prospective studies to investigate behavioural change. In Strauss, J. S., Babigian, H. M. and Roff, M. (eds) *Methods of Longitudinal Research in Psychopathology*. New York: Plenum Publishing.

Rutter, M. (1978) Family, area and school influence in the genesis of conduct disorders. In Hersov, L., Berger, M and Schaffer, D. (eds) *Aggression and anti-social behaviour in childhood and adolescence*. Oxford: Pergamon.

Rutter, M. and Graham, P. (1968) The reliability and validity of the psychiatric assessment of the child: I. Interview with the child, *Brit. J. Psychiat.* 114, 563–79.

Rutter, M., Lebovici, S., Eisenberg, L., Snerzevskij, A. V., Sadoun, R., Broke, E. and Tsun, Yi Lin (1969) A triaxial classification of mental disorders in children, *J. Child Psychol. Psychiat.* 10, 41–61.

Rutter, M., Tizard, J. and Whitmore, K. (eds) (1970) *Education, Health and Behaviour*. London: Longman.

Rutter, M., Yule, W., Berger, M., Yule, B., Morton, J. and Bagley, C. (1974) Children of West Indian immigrants: I. Rates of behavioural deviance and of psychiatric disorder, *J. Child Psychol. Psychiat.* 15, 241–62.

Rutter, M., Cox, A., Tupling, C., Berger, M. and Yule, W. (1975a) Attainment and adjustment in two geographical areas: I. The prevalence of psychiatric disorders, *Brit. J. Psychiat.* 126, 493–509.

Rutter, M., Yule, B., Quinton, D., Rowlands, O., Yule, W. and Berger, M. (1975b) Attainment and adjustment in two geographical areas: III. Some factors accounting for area differences. *Brit. J. Psychiat.* 126, 520–33.

Rutter, M., Yule, B., Morton, J. and Bagley, C. (1975c) Children of West Indian immigrants: III. Home circumstances and family patterns, *J. Child Psychol. Psychiat.* **16**, 105–23.

Rutter, M., Graham, P., Chadwick, O. F. D. and Yule, W. (1976) Adolescent turmoil: fact or fiction, *J. Child Psychol. Psychiat.* **17**, 35–56.

Rutter, M. and Quinton, D. (1977) Psychiatric disorder – ecological factors and concepts of causation. In: McGurk, H. (ed.) *Ecological Factors in Human Development*. Amsterdam: North-Holland.

Rutter, M., Maughan, B., Mortimore, P., Ouston, J. and Smith, A. (1979) *Fifteen Thousand Hours: Secondary Schools and their Effects on Pupils*. London: Open Books.

Scottish Education Department (1977) *Truancy and Indiscipline in Schools in Scotland* (The Pack Report). London: HMSO.

Shepherd, M., Oppenheim, B. and Mitchell, S. (1971) *Childhood Behaviour and Mental Health*. London: University of London Press.

Simpson, J. (1962) Sickness absence in teachers, *British Journal of Industrial Medicine* **19**, 110–15.

Spiers vs. *Warrington Corporation* (1954). Law Reports, 1 QB, 61–70. 1 QB 61.

Stott, D. H. (1963) *The Social Adjustment of Children*. 2nd edn, London: Univ. of London Press.

Taylor, M., Miller, J. and Oliveira, M. (1979) The off-site unit, *Comprehensive Education* **39**, No. 375, 13–17.

Tyerman, M. J. (1968) *Truancy*. London: Univ. of London Press.

Uger, C. (1938) The relationship of teachers' attitudes to children's problem behaviour, *School and Society*, **47**, 246–8.

Vacc, N. A. (1968) A study of emotionally disturbed children in regular and special classes, *Exceptional Children* **35**, 197–204.

Vacc, N. A. (1972) Long term effects of special class intervention for emotionally disturbed children, *Exceptional Children* **39**, September, 15–22.

Ward, J. (1971) Modification of deviant classroom behaviour, *Brit. J. Educ. Psychol.* **41**, 304–13.

Wechsler, D. (1949) *Wechsler Intelligence Scale for Children* (Manual). New York: The Psychological Corporation.

Werthman, C. (1963) Delinquents in schools: a test for the legitimacy of authority, *Berkeley Journal of Sociology* **8**, 39–60.

West, D. J. and Farrington, D. (1973) *Who Becomes Delinquent?* London: Heinemann.

White, R. and Brockington, D. (1978) *In and Out of School: The ROSLA Community Education Project*. London: Routledge and Kegan Paul.

Whitmore, K. (1974) The contribution of child guidance to the community, *Occasional Paper 2*. London: MIND.

Wilcox, B. and Eustace, P. J. (1980) *Tooling up for Curriculum Review*. Windsor: NFER.

Williams, P. (1974) The growth and scope of the school psychological service. In: Chazan, M., Moore, T., Williams, P. and Wright, J. (eds) *The Practice of Educational Psychology*. London: Longman.

Wills, D. (1941) *The Hawkspur Experiment*. London: Allen and Unwin.

Wolf, M. M., Phillips, E. L. and Fixsen, D. L. (1975) *Achievement Place Phase II: Final Report*. Dept. of Human Development, University of Kansas.

Wright, D. M., Moelis, I. and Pollack, L. J. (1976) The outcome of individual child psychotherapy: increments at follow-up, *J. Child Psychol. Psychiat.* **17**, 275–85.

York, R., Heron, J. M. and Wolff, S. (1972) Exclusion from school, *J. Child Psychol. Psychiat.* **13**, 259–66.

Yule, W. (1978) Behavioural treatment of children and adolescents with conduct disorders. In: Hersov, L., Berger, M. and Schaffer, D. (eds) *Aggression and Anti-social Behaviour in Childhood and Adolescence*. Oxford: Pergamon.

Yule, W., Berger, M., Rutter, M. and Yule, B. (1975) Children of West Indian immigrants: II. Intellectual performance and reading attainment, *J. Child Psychol. Psychiat.* **16**, 1–17.

Index